GOLF

FROM

The Times

Welcome to the Rare Book Collection, a unique compilation of golfing history proudly presented by Sports Media Group.

If you are interested enough in the game to be reading this page, you are likely aware of golf's matchless position within the library of sport, a standing supported by a body of international writing as richly varied as it is venerated. Indeed, with aspects as wide-ranging as instruction, history, course architecture, biographies, travel, tournament play, and all manner of fine anthologies, the field of golf literature has, for nearly 300 years, provided us with exceptional prose in areas far more diverse than any other game.

The goal of the Rare Book Collection is a simple one: To provide, at affordable prices, quality reprints of coveted golf volumes that, through scarcity or prohibitive cost, have heretofore lay beyond the reach of many readers. Our list of titles is uncommonly broad, its authors representing a veritable Who's Who from the game's long and storied past. It features many acknowledged classics but also a variety of hidden gems, overlooked or forgotten works every bit as interesting to mainstream readers as they are to serious collectors. Above all, it is our purpose to revive these great works at an attractive price, making the game's greatest—and rarest—titles available at a cost affordable to readers worldwide.

As coeditors of the Rare Book Collection, we enjoy the unique privilege of helping to select these volumes, and to reintroduce them with brief historical notes. We join everyone at Sports Media Group in hoping that you will gain as much enjoyment from reading these timeless works as we have in selecting and publishing them.

Daniel Wexler
Mel Lucas

Editor's Note

Within the vast body of golf literature, one of my very favorite introductory sentences comes from the noted British poet/ writer Patric Dickinson who, in his 1952 volume *A Round of Golf Courses*, begins a chapter on the Old Course by observing: "There is nothing new to say about St. Andrews, just as there is nothing new to say about ShakespEditor's Noteeare." A splendid opener and one that, I believe, applies equally well to the work of the great Bernard Darwin. For how much is there really new to say about golf's most chronicled writer some 43 years after his death?

Before offering at least a modest answer, a bit of background information is in order—though with readers who seek out so rare a collection as this likely knowing a thing or two of Darwin's life already, we shall keep it brief.

The grandson of the legendary evolutionist Charles Darwin, Bernard Richard Meirion Darwin was born in Downe, England (just southeast of London) on September 7, 1876. A fine player from an early age, he first attended Eton College, then Cambridge University where he captained the golf team and graduated in 1897. Initially pursuing a career in law, he was called to the British bar in 1903 but having dabbled a bit in writing, soon found that medium far more to his liking. Thus in 1907 he turned to writing full time, thereafter maintaining simultaneous careers with the *Times* and *Country Life* that would last for nearly half a century.

Like his disciple Henry Longhurst, Darwin was a bit of an old-timer whose traditional values could ruffle the occasional feather, such as when he chastised 1951 Open champion Max Faulkner for interrupting his conversation, saying "Don't you realize, Faulkner, that I am talking to a *gentleman*?" He was also, by most accounts, a highly competitive sort who, if not participating, took a great rooting interest in even the smallest contests—a circumstance that perhaps explains his daunting on-course temper. Yet despite such partisanship and volatility, Darwin's writing possessed only an engagingly pleasant dose of "rooting" and, given its decidedly agreeable tone, was much the better for it.

As a competitor Darwin is, I believe, terribly underrated, often being written off under the overly broad heading "good amateur player." But in truth he was quite a bit more, representing England in her "international" matches with Scotland on eight occasions and winning such prominent amateur competitions as the *Golf Illustrated* Gold Vase in 1919, the Oxford & Cambridge Golfing Society's President's Putter in 1924, and the Worplesdon Foursomes (with no less than Joyce Wethered) in 1933. More impressively, he twice reached the semifinals of the British Amateur, losing to eventual champions Robert Maxwell (in 1909 at Muirfield) and Willie Hunter (in 1921 at Hoylake). But Darwin's competitive zenith surely came in 1922 while covering the inaugural Walker Cup match at the National Golf Links of America when, as the only extra Briton on hand, he was asked to replace team captain Robert Harris who had suddenly fallen ill. Darwin obligingly teamed with Cyril Tolley to lose a foursomes match against Francis Ouimet and Jess Guilford, then rose up in singles to defeat 1910 U.S. Amateur champion William Fownes 3 and 1.

More than 30 volumes have come into print bearing Darwin's name, most of them immensely enjoyable anthologies of his newspaper and magazine work. In addition, several of his full-length manuscripts stand out as genuine classics including *Green Memories* (Hodder & Stoughton, 1928), *Golf Between Two Wars* (Chatto & Windus, 1944), and the seminal *Golf Courses of the British Isles* (Duckworth, 1910). Darwin also penned one golf biography, *James Braid* (Hodder & Stoughton, 1952) as well as several autobiographical works, and was a primary contributor to one of the truly great historical volumes, *A History of Golf in Britain* (Cassell, 1952).

The most amazing aspect of our continuing adoration of his work, I think, is that it continues despite the obviously dated nature of the material. For while titles like *Green Memories* and *Golf Between Two Wars* stand up nicely as straight historical volumes, the many Darwin anthologies contain only newspaper and/or magazine pieces highlighting people, places, and events from five to nine decades ago. Indeed, even the landmark *Golf Courses of the British*

Isles became outdated enough—by 1925!—to require a substantially revised second edition.*

So why, given its limited relevance, do we remain so passionately drawn to this work?

The answer, I believe, lies in several unique qualities of Darwin's writing. To begin with, he possessed a profound, almost visceral knowledge of the game and its myriad pitfalls and splendors, a depth of understanding that was likely approached by Herbert Warren Wind and Henry Longhurst (along with one or two other postwar Britons) but which is almost completely lacking in our modern coverage of the game.

Of comparable importance, I think, is the matchless breadth of Darwin's span, for this was a man who saw every great player from Willie Park Jr. and John Ball to Ben Hogan and Jack Nicklaus, a more than 60-year window dating back to an otherwise largely undocumented time. Indeed, in writing my own encyclopedic volume *The Book of Golfers*, I discovered many an early player for whom the only truly cogent description was Darwin's, for nobody else (with the occasional exception of Horace Hutchinson) was seriously plying the field before World War I.

But most frequently cited, of course, is Darwin's writing style, a splendidly easy, almost conversational manner that was at once welcoming in the ease of its tone, yet of an impeccable grammatical and linguistic standard. He also managed that wonderful achievement of conveying great detail without ever losing pace, an accomplishment aided partially by our happy willingness to ride along during his always entertaining diversions, but also, I suspect, by the great ambience of his work. For Darwin's prose was so steeped in golf—its history and nuances in addition to the fundamental challenge of putting club to ball—that we feel, upon opening the cover, as if we are stepping directly into his world. Thus even when only minimal detail is provided, our imaginations can do the rest, placing us squarely in a golfing landscape so much simpler and, in many ways, richer than the game's contemporary milieu.

Darwin's world is one to which any true golfer enjoys returning, though I fear it now teeters on the edge of extinction. The game as he knew it has been sadly compromised by our modern emphasis on technology over skill, obsessions with course rankings, and a generally crass commercialism which justifies pretty much anything so long as the goal is a good, honest profit (frequently hidden, I might add, behind that wonderfully ambiguous phrase "growing the game").

And therein lies the crux of the deal. To the modern golfer, for whom nirvana is driving the ball 320 equipment-enhanced yards and having a GPS system relay exact distances to their golf cart, Darwin's influence is, I suspect, a fleeting one. But for those more in tune with golf's underlying greatness—its inherent variety and strategies, the vagaries of courses and techniques, the fundamental essence of the unceasing challenge—Darwin's words become timeless for they speak, with uncommon eloquence, to the very core of the game's greatness. For that golfer (whose numbers, I fear, are dwindling), Darwin's words simply *are* golf. They have never been bettered.

In this light, the book you are about to read is really quite important for several reasons. To begin with, its 1912 appearance makes it Darwin's second published anthology—though in my estimation, it was the first of real significance as its predecessor, *Tee Shots and Others* (1911), was composed of rather ill-defined material culled from at least four different publications. This volume, on the other hand, comes entirely from the *Times* and thus represents the true beginning of Darwin's work as it would generally come to be known. Second, *Golf from the Times* is, as its subtitle suggests, "A Reprint, revised and re-arranged, of some articles on golf." The accent here must be placed on "revised and re-arranged," for this text has been heavily reconfigured into ten full-sized chapters, thus reading far more like an original manuscript than the random collection of pieces that inhabit most Darwin anthologies. And finally there is the book's utter scarcity, for this is not only Darwin's most elusive anthology but also one of his rarest titles altogether, making its reprint by the Rare Book Collection a real godsend for Darwin fans—and real golfers—everywhere.

Daniel Wexler

Golf Courses of the British Isles is a very hard-to-find volume soon to be reprinted, I am proud to say, by the Rare Book Collection.

G O L F

FROM

𝕿𝖍𝖊  𝕿𝖎𝖒𝖊𝖘

A Reprint, revised and
re-arranged, of some
Articles on Golf, by
𝕿𝖍𝖊 𝕿𝖎𝖒𝖊𝖘
Special Contributor.

SMG
SPORTS
MEDIA
GROUP

Facsimile reprint of 1912 edition
Printed by John Parkinson Bland,
at "The Times" Office.
Printing House Square, E.C.

All inquiries should be addressed to:
Sports Media Group
An imprint of Ann Arbor Media Group LLC
2500 S. State Street
Ann Arbor, MI 48104

Printed and bound at Edwards Brothers, Inc.,
Lillington, North Carolina, USA

08   07   06   05   04   1   2   3   4   5

ISBN 1-58726-175-8

CONTENTS.

PREFACE.

The following papers have no educational mission. They consist of reflections, somewhat at random, upon various aspects of the game, and make only this claim on the reader's consideration—that the writer has had the opportunity of seeing much of the best and most interesting golf played during the last few years. Indeed, it is likely that the influence of some recent event, the transient enthusiasm inspired now by this champion and now by that, will be detected here and there in what has been written. Since the memory of a great match, even amongst those who saw it, is apt to become sadly blurred by time, a chapter has been added containing reports of a few recent matches which may justifiably be called historic.

The Times
BOOK OF GOLF.

I.

ON THE MAKING OF COURSES IN GENERAL.

Among the arguments, some excellent and some not at all convincing, which are advanced in favour of a standard ball is one that gives rise to some interesting speculations. It is alleged that those who lay out courses, in straining every nerve to outwit the resilient and far-flying ball, have ended by making holes that are worthy of the name of trickery rather than that of golf, and have allowed artifice to supplant Nature to far too great an extent. This statement has a plausible sound and has, at any rate, one valuable piece of support in the words of a very skilful and well-known " architect," who, in speaking of a certain course, expressed the hope that it would, by reason of its difficulties, " get even with the ball makers." Yet it may be argued with some show of reason that it is not the modern ball that is wholly responsible for the trend of modern " architecture," and that either the distinguished gentleman in question has been misunderstood or he did not fully appreciate his own motives or the evolution of his own art.

It may freely be granted that there is sometimes a tendency to mistake trickiness for genuine difficulty; it generally shows itself in the excessive slopes on the putting green, whereby a perfectly innocent person may be left with a put which he may conceivably hole but cannot by anything short of a miracle lay dead. Apart from such antics as these sheer difficulty can be, and is, occasionally overdone. When, without any antecedent mistake on the player's part, the ball has to be artificially sliced or hooked in order to attain its goal it is at least arguable that matters have gone too far. But are these occasional aberrations of a skilful and ingenious race really due to the ball? Are they not merely due to an exuberance which must be almost inevitable in any art which is young and progressive—and the designing of golf courses is surely worthy to be described both by that noun and by its two attendant epithets.

If golfers still played with gutty balls and Mr. Haskell had never conferred on them the exceedingly dubious benefit of his invention, their courses would not, it is needless to say, be as they are now. They would be different in one obvious respect in that they would not be so long. But before the rubber-cored ball came in, the laying-out of courses was recognized as a matter for much skill and meditation, and was no longer merely a rule of thumb affair. The more thoughtful among golfers had already begun to analyse the holes that they deemed the best, and had come to certain conclusions founded on that analysis; they had, for instance, begun to instil into less imaginative minds a new conception of the purport and functions of a bunker. They had pointed out—and Mr. John Low was particularly eloquent in this respect—that it was not the whole end and object of a bunker only to punish a hopelessly bad stroke and never in any circumstances to catch any other stroke ; that the best bunker was the one that insisted on a reasonable measure of risk being taken, even by a good player hitting his ball reasonably well. It is not intended to say, of course, that no one among the older golfers had ever hit on this truth before ; only that the artistic and scientific designing of courses came to be much more deeply and more widely considered, and that a little while before the advent of the rubber ball. It was, if memory serves, before that most unfortunate year of 1902 that Mr. Low was instrumental in cutting in the 17th green at Woking two pot bunkers, one of which still bears his name in affectionate remembrance. Certainly the members gaped in some amazement at a bunker cut in their finest and most velvety stretch of green, and grumbled more than they would now in similar circumstances ; they were less severely educated than they are to-day, but the process of breaking them in had begun.

So here were ready all the elements of a great change in the making of courses—" architects " full of enthusiasm and new theories, their victims beginning dimly to apprehend their meaning and not wholly disapproving of it. If there had been no change of ball, those enthusiastic builders of courses would surely not have stood still ; they would have gone on their way rejoicing in each new difficulty they devised, and they would have made courses far better, more difficult, and more interesting than they were before, just as they have done now. Apart from the obvious point of length, there is doubtless one other point in which the ball has played an important part. Bunkers have to be put very close to the holes to-day, because the green is so constantly approached with an iron club, which is comparatively an accurate weapon. If, as in the romantic past, the golfer had often to hit a full brassy shot up to the hole, he would rightly insist on having his greens less congested with bunkers. Nevertheless, one ventures to assert that, even had the gutty ball remained, progressive designers would by this time have got their bunkers just as near to the holes as they dared, and a great deal nearer than was pleasant to many golfers ; there would have been the same struggles and the same compromises between victim and executioner.

It is sometimes said that the laying out of courses is becoming too artificial ; and it is at least true that whole forests are cut down to make way for plateaux and hollows and mountain ranges in a manner that was once undreamed of. Also it is obviously true that there is a unique charm about an unartificial course, and that a bunker or a plateau made by Nature's hand is worth more than the most elaborate and beautiful creation. But what is man to do when Nature declines to stir hand or foot to help him ? Is he to become fulsome over the beauties of a flat field, a hedge, a ditch, and possibly a hay-stack ? That is where he will get to if he goes logically back to Nature.

One specific charge of artificiality is sometimes levelled at the designer's head in respect to " dog-leg " holes. Suppose there is on the route to the hole some such hazard as a wood or a mass of whins, it is said that the designer, instead of allowing the golfer to swipe manfully and straightforwardly over the wood, drags him back to a tee whence he cannot carry the hazard, and so must play round it, a " dog-leg " hole being thus introduced and a good many yards added on to the total length of the course. In this accusation there is doubtless some truth, and it would be a sad pity if one was never again allowed the fearful joy of hitting over such a hazard as that sea of rushes at the 10th hole at Westward Ho ! But the " dog-leg " is also an admirable hole, and it is altogether too natural and primitive to demand that the golfer shall necessarily walk forward and not back to his tee. It would be much nicer if he could always go forward, since there is a feeling of artificiality about walking back merely to gain in length ; but to arrange a course on those principles at this time of day would be too consciously unsophisticated and archaic, and the course would probably be a bad one into the bargain. Moreover, it can hardly be said against the designers of to-day that they wilfully refuse to avail themselves of any scrap of help that Nature gives them. Where they differ from some of their critics is in their attitude of mind ; they deem a hindrance what the critic thinks a help, and that is a difference that nothing can compose.

Whether or not they are too much inclined towards artificiality in their methods, modern " architects " have at any rate made very good and very difficult courses : so difficult that the majority of golfers, whose drives are short and whose handicaps are long, occasionally cry out in anguish. It is, for example, interesting to observe that the members of the Hythe Golf Club, having some while since had their course made longer and more difficult, have now deliberately abandoned some of the new holes and difficulties and returned to the course which they knew, and apparently loved, before.) The members of the Richmond Club, again, who play their golf in that most charming of spots, Sudbrook Park, resolved by a large majority to have nothing to do with a scheme for the reconstruction of their course, put forward by one not only of the most distinguished, but also of the most sane and reasonable of golfing " architects." For some time past such a revolution has, half in jest, been prophesied, and now the thing has happened in real earnest. Whether these two are isolated outbreaks, or whether the revolt will spread from course to course, it will be in the highest degree entertaining to observe.

So far as can be judged from one or two of the newest and best of inland courses, some of those who design them have heard the rumble of the distant thunder and, in a measure at least, bowed their heads to the storm before it is actually upon them. They continue with wholly unabated energy to make the life of the good player a burden, but they are coming more and more to treat the weaker player with an indifference bordering upon contempt—an insult which the latter will swallow with grateful humility. Thus the bunkers for the tee shot are almost always designed with a view to those who can drive a reasonably long ball; the short driver may have to carry a certain distance over heather, but the flanking bunkers, set on the edges of the fairway, are as often as not wholly outside the range of practical politics so far as his tee shot is concerned. It follows that as regards the two-shot holes—and a two-shot hole to-day means one well over four hundred yards in length—the bunkers close to the green should lose for the short driver many of their terrors. He cannot reach them with his two shots which bring him within comfortable approaching range of the green ; and so has only to encounter with a mashie those perils that have to be faced with a brassey or a cleek by his more arrogant and long-driving brother. One should make his jog-trot journey in an inglorious security; the other has his heart in his mouth all the way. Both parties should be satisfied and the " architect's " life be safe.

The long handicap player should have no real grievance as to the longer holes, unless he complain of mere length in itself; the laugh on the whole is with him. But perhaps it is not the long holes but the short ones that will be the cause of the revolution if it comes. No course is to-day thought properly equipped without four or five one-shot holes, all of a more or less hazardous character, and there are very few drivers so short or so humble that they will make it the summit of their ambition to reach a one-shot hole in two strokes. These short holes, designed as a rule with terrible ingenuity, are difficult for the superior being who can reach them with a half-iron shot ; to him the bunkers appear huddled round the green in the most ample profusion. What must those bunkers look like to the man who has to hit his hardest with a wooden club ? Moreover, in this instance no compromise seems to be possible. A long hole may be flat and easy and dull, but at any rate there is some satisfaction in opening the shoulders ; a short hole without a considerable spice of danger must, one would think, be the dullest and most depressing of all conceivable holes, even from the standpoint of the humblest players. So, if the short holes are complained of, the revolutionaries should most easily be satisfied by the courses being made still longer than they are at present, a pleasing and paradoxical conclusion to the whole affair.

The poor architect, while he has to be as sympathetic as possible to the weak player, must not be too kind-hearted. He must try in some measure to prevent the ever-increasing running powers of the rubber-cored ball from making his courses ridiculously easy. There are some people who think that this object can be effected not by altering the character of the ball itself, but by a lavish display of cross-bunkers.

At the first glance the scheme appears to be well worth a trial, because the small heavy ball, which is the cause of all the pother, goes such prodigious distances, chiefly owing to its powers of running. If the players could be compelled to devote more of their attention to carry and so to hit a higher ball from the tee, it would appear that they would lose so much in the matter of run that the total length of their drives would be appreciably lessened. In making this statement one must assume that with the small heavy ball the character of driving has in a measure changed, and that the longest drivers have learnt to hit a lower and less carrying ball than they did, in order to take full advantage of the run. In golf, as in everything else, it is so hard to remember exactly what used to happen a year or two ago that one cannot but profoundly distrust one's own judgment on such a point. However, a very distinguished professional has assured the writer that the professionals have in fact perceptibly modified their method of driving in quite recent times, and this is an opinion difficult to disregard.

So far, so good, although the professionals are

not the only golfers, and other people can, in proportion at any rate, hit the ball a long way. The difficulty—and it seems almost an insurmountable one—lies in the immobile character of a cross-bunker, which cannot be in two places at once. The bunker placed in such a position as to compel Braid, for example, to hit a higher and more carrying ball would be so situated that comparatively few players could carry it at all; the highly respectable drive would find a sandy grave time after time and the highly respectable driver be compelled to take a cleek from the tee. In a lower stratum of golfing society exactly the same thing would occur; the bunker that made the short handicap player think would make his long handicap friend weep in impotent despair. It may be urged that for the golfer to be compelled to use his head in discerning when to play short is admirable discipline, and there is little to be said against this argument save that the golfer will not stand it for a moment; what he wants to use is not his own head, but that of his longest wooden club. It is, therefore, not so much a question as to which particular class of players is to be slightly curbed in the exuberance of its hitting, but as to which class is to lose most of its pleasure in the game. Until a cross-bunker can be devised possessed of some properties not at present known to exist in inanimate objects the scheme can hardly be an effective one.

The future of the cross-bunker seems to lie in other directions than that of shortening the tee shot. For one thing, certain old-established cross-bunkers, having passed through a period of obloquy and contempt, are now once more admitted to serve a useful purpose, although it is a purpose rather different from that originally intended. Once designed to be pitched over with the third stroke, they have now come to be interesting obstacles for the second.

The bunker that guards the 13th hole at Sandwich may be given as a fair example. Originally, although mighty hitters might occasionally reach the green in two, for the ordinary mortal two good shots were needed in order to obtain position near the bunker and duly pitch over it with the third. Then came the rubber-cored ball, which went just so far that it was easy to get into the bunker in two shots and very, very difficult to get over it; the result was that the second stroke for the vast majority of players was an exceedingly dull one with an iron, having all the demerits of a stroke played short with no compensating advantages. Now the ball goes yet a little further and the hole is changed once more, so that it is with a pardonable triumph that the eminent gentleman who originally designed it points to the vindication of his calumniated bunker. At the Open Championship at Sandwich in 1911 he joyfully watched player after player getting home on to the green in two good strokes, of which the second was often played with an iron club; and the hole was certainly as good an one as might be.

A few old bunkers on old courses may in this way come to their own again, but looking at the new courses it would seem that the chief purpose of the cross-bunker is to be the very proper one of teasing the indifferent pitcher beyond endurance. The drive-and-pitch hole came into such general contempt not, as was often alleged, because it was of a bad length, but because the bunkers were placed at just such a distance from the hole as to do the minimum of harm to any human creature. It was said, and quite truly, that the man who hit a bad tee shot was scarcely a bit the worse, since he could still get up comfortably enough by taking a longer club for his second. He would not have been so contented with his lot, however, nor would his long-driving adversary have been so discontented, if the bunker had been quite close to the hole instead of 60 yards away from it. If only the bunker is near enough to the hole, the man who has hit a short tee shot is adequately punished, because he cannot with his second make his ball stop upon the green.

This, however, is only, as it were, a negative merit; the positive merit of the cross-bunker close to the hole is that a really difficult pitch, in which the ball has to be played quite straight and with a measure of cut, is a most attractive stroke. To hit hard is always more or less entertaining, but a gentle stroke only becomes amusing when it is really difficult. There is a hole at Northwood, called appropriately " Death or Glory," which, in spite of more than a suspicion of muddiness and a very ordinary tee shot, is made really thrilling by the second, a fairly short mashie shot. To mention two courses quite lately laid out, Mr. Fowler has made two holes at Delamere Forest and Mr. Colt one at Swinley Forest wherein the second shot is a pitch the very shortest possible; yet in each case the ball must be pitched such a little way over a bunker, and must stop so quickly on the other side, that the stroke is truly alarming. At such holes as these almost anything that is unpleasant may happen to the bad pitcher—the man who cannot hit his ball crisply as well as delicately. He may half top his ball with the broad sole of his niblick, so that it flies an incredible distance over

the green, or, which is even more likely, he may
" fluff " it ignominiously so short a distance that
he has still the bunker between him and the
hole. In fact, in these cases it is only a very
small part of the bunker's functions actually to
catch the erring ball ; it is there to frighten its
victim into some less obvious mistake and to
repay the player who can cut his ball with a
mashie and not merely shovel it into the air
with a niblick. If it be only near enough to
the hole it performs both functions admirably.

When the harassed player has pitched safely
over the bunker and his ball is lying tolerably near
the hole, he will find that on many modern courses
his troubles are by no means over yet. He
has still to reckon with the " architect's " pretty
and occasionally fantastic taste in undulations.

The putting green becomes with the opening of
each new course a more complex and ingenious
work of art. It may be said with comparatively
little exaggeration that at one time the maker
of golf courses selected for his green the flattest
and smoothest piece of turf he could find. Next
he rolled it until he had smoothed out such
natural wrinkles as were in it ; finally, as Yankee
Doodle " stuck a feather in his cap and called
it macaroni," so he stuck a flag in the middle
and called it a putting green. This procedure
was occasionally varied by the selection of a deep
little dell or hollow, having this charming
property, that a ball once in it could never get
out again ; thus approach shots, good, bad, or
indifferent, all served almost equally well their
ultimate purpose.

A sloping putting green was, as a rule, a thing
of beautiful simplicity in that it all sloped one
way. Fearful stories were told of two players
standing at the bottom of such a green and

having alternate puts at the hole; they had no need materially to change their positions, since the ball, having evaded the hole, rolled gently down hill again to the spot whence it started and the hole was in the end halved by mutual consent. It may be remembered that a somewhat similar incident occurred in the final match of the London Amateur Foursomes Tournament not very long ago, when, on a day of piercing east wind and hard, glassy greens, each side reached the tenth green at Walton Heath in one stroke and each ultimately conceded the other a half in five. Greens of this character used formerly to be found in large numbers upon downland courses, and when at last they earned a well-merited unpopularity they were succeeded by something hardly less hateful, flat greens built out of the hillside, having on one side a back-wall of chalk and on the other a precipitous drop.

These things have now for the most part passed away, and the maker of golf courses goes to work in a far more scientific manner. He may be pictured sitting in his study with a bare wooden board in front of him and a far-away look in his eyes, evolving from his inner consciousness the slopes and counter-slopes of the perfect putting green. When the vision comes to him he dashes at the board in a kind of ecstasy and deftly models his miniature putting green upon it in green " plasticine "—graceful curves and hog's-back ridges that shall kick away from the hole the ball that is not perfectly struck and bunkers in ambush behind the ridges to consummate the disaster. By this means he not only evolves greens which are entertaining, sometimes almost to the point of aggravation, but he saves himself many of the troubles of an overseer and ensures that his design shall be carried out as he intended; for it appears that a workman can imitate a model far more effectively than he can work from an ordinary plan, even if reinforced by oral directions.

It is clear that the undulating green is open to abuses; the hand of the designer must be skilful and the undulations must not be overdone. Again, the designer has to consider all reasonable kinds of weather, and the put that is both fair and interesting in winter may become farcical in an ordinarily dry summer. Finally, there is an increased responsibility on the greenkeeper, for it is possible by a display of quite ordinary stupidity in cutting the hole immediately at the foot of a slope to give to one man a hopeless put downhill, and to his opponent, who has done nothing to deserve it, a back-wall that shall double his chance of holing out. Dangers must, however, always attend the exaggeration of any good quality, and the greater number of the undulating greens of to-day probably add to the legitimate interest of the game.

The designer, moreover, is an infinitely resourceful person, and is constantly inventing fresh varieties of undulation, of which specimens may be seen on the different sandy courses that now cluster round London. At the 4th hole at Swinley Forest, for example, there is a most ingenious preventive of the back-wall policy. The green can be reached with a good iron shot from the tee, and, since there is a wall of turf behind the green, it would seem at first sight that the player might play too strong a stroke with the certain knowledge that the ball would rebound into the middle of the green. But at the foot of the wall there is a moderately deep trough or dip in the green, and it is there that the ball will lie, so that the player will have a most difficult put out of a valley and over the crest of a ridge—a just and moderate penalty for the exuberance of his tee shot.

The 15th hole at Woking may be quoted as a good example of what can be done with a green that was by nature quite dull and flat and lacking in distinction. First of all from out the level plain there arose a long, narrow little plateau, and when the hole was cut on this plateau it was quite possible with a little misdirected energy to put from the lowlands on one side on to the lowlands on the other. This was felt to be somewhat too exacting, and so the plateau has been lowered and other gentle hills and shallow valleys have gradually come into being around it, until the whole green is now one network of ingenious slopes.

Certainly one of the very best of artificial plateau greens is to be found at the 13th hole at Westward Ho !, where in the midst of a flat expanse a small tableland rises so naturally and gently as most effectually to conceal the art of the maker. Of a rather different type and of less recent invention, but also very interesting in their own way, are those imitations of the " Pandy " green at Musselburgh which are to be found at Worplesdon and Huntercombe.

Woking may lay claim to one excellent and original device in the mountain range that divides the 7th green into two distinct compartments. This is a one-shot hole, and almost any stroke not atrociously bad ought to reach some part of the green, which is a large one ; but there is a vast difference between being in the haven of rest, the right compartment with a possible put for a 2, and in the wrong compartment, with a mountain intervening betwixt ball and hole and a rather remote chance of a 3. This plan has been adopted and probably improved upon in the 13th green at Swinley Forest, where the dividing chain of hills is not so tall as that at Woking, but full of a greater and more puzzling variety of slopes. This short list of examples might very easily be multiplied, and even so the last word in undulating greens, and for that matter in ingenious " architecture " generally, has doubtless not yet been said.

II

SOME COURSES IN PARTICULAR.

A very good and experienced golfer once remarked to the writer that he did not much care for playing upon courses that were strange to him, because the chief pleasure in golf consisted in knowing exactly what had to be done and then in trying to do it. This observation fell from him very soon after he had played an apparently admirable pitching shot, only to see his ball " dunt " heavily into the face of a little hill and then totter slowly backwards until it reposed in a hollow some 15 yards short of the flag ; had he known the course he would almost certainly have played a running shot and the ball would have clambered gaily up the hill and lain near the hole. Still, he spoke in so entirely calm and judicial a spirit that one could not for a moment suspect the criticism of being biassed by mere passing events, and the standpoint which it discloses is an interesting one. It is also rather a lofty one, to which all golfers cannot aspire, befitting a player who has such control over his clubs as to be able to take advantage of every turn and twist of the ground, and especially one who has spent much of his golfing life in coping with the banks and braes of St. Andrews.

To hold these views is to miss or, at any rate, minimize a good deal of enjoyment, because there is to most people much of both interest and pleasure in playing over new courses, if these are at all worthy of a name that is too often profaned. At the same time it must be admitted that the fun of playing over a new course is different from that to be obtained upon some happy hunting ground. In both cases there are many occasions when the plain, honest clean-hit stroke is all that is needed and reaps a due reward, nor are there many golfers who are so familiar with it as wholly to despise it ; but in the finer points of approaching it is only the well-known course that can give the most exquisite thrill, a difficulty exactly understood and overcome by exactly the means intended. On the strange course the absolutely honest player will often have to confess that the most that ought to be said for him is that he guessed right.

Courses vary very greatly in the amount of difficulty that they present to the stranger. Those which are generally praised with such epithets as " jolly "—the courses of glorious carries over big hills and gloriously big putting greens—as a rule treat the visitor rather kindly. There are, it is true, apt to be a good many blind strokes, but a blind stroke with a wooden club is not a very difficult matter to a stranger ; he has a splendid singleness of purpose, since he has but one thing on which to concentrate his attention, a guide flag or a caddie's head. It is to be sure a very different thing when the blind stroke is not a full one, for to play an iron shot of imperfectly defined length into space is as difficult as it is dull. Those courses, on the other hand, which earn the praises of the sterner moralists are, as a rule, terribly puzzling on a first visit. They have probably very few blind holes—indeed,

it is in a large measure on that account that the
more rigid will allow them to be golf courses at
all—but they possess the cunningest little
plateaux, hogs' backs, runs, and kicks that are
far more disturbing ; also they have occasionally
a bunker hidden behind a brae at just that
particular spot where the guileless stranger
would least expect to find it. Much more
deceitful than either are the courses that lie
on sloping, wind-swept downs, where the greens
are as the roofs of houses, unless, indeed, they
rather resemble a rackets court with one wall
missing ; on such courses the local hero is practically invulnerable, and his victim had better
take the high line and deny the initial proposition that they are golf courses.

Golfers, of course, differ enormously in the skill
with which they can wrestle with a new course,
but those who have played over many courses are
perhaps a little prone to forget that experience
has a vast deal to do with it. When Mr. Abe
Mitchell went to Hoylake for the Amateur
Championship of 1909 he met with a sand
bunker for the first time in his life, and for a day
or two the bunkers had by far the best of the
encounter, since his native course of Ashdown
Forest possesses a great variety of hazards, but
not one particle of sand. It says much for his great
natural abilities that he overcame so brilliantly
difficulties which it is rather hard for most golfers
to realize, since there are few of them so inexperienced or so blameless as not at some time
or other to have found their ball in sand. Hardly
any substance upon which golf is played can by
this time be strange to the leading professionals,
and the way in which they can grapple with a new
situation is extraordinary. They suffer, moreover, from the additional difficulty that an

ordinary caddie's advice is likely to be still more grossly misleading to them than to humbler players, even if they have a kind of rough sliding scale in their heads on which to work, taking a cleek if they are offered a brassey, and so on. In watching them play on some course where the caddies are rather rudimentary one may observe that they depend less on oral advice than on the length of the holes as given on the scoring card. In order to do this they have to know roughly how many yards they can compass with any particular kind of stroke, and this is a valuable bit of knowledge, since, amongst other things, it must minimize the deceitfulness of appearances as regards distance. It is one which many a good amateur player does not possess ; he knows vaguely the look of the distance that he can compass with a particular club, but could not state it at all accurately in yards.

It is something of a truism that one's first round over a fresh course is likely to be better than one's second or even one's third. In the first round ignorance is sometimes bliss, and the player may all unknowing take the most hideous risks with perfect success and without turning a hair. Nevertheless he would be a bold man who should act up to this common belief and deliberately abstain from a practice round in order to come to the course in absolute ignorance rather than with a half understanding of its perils. There was once a golfer who, being offered by a stranger the five strokes that constituted his legal allowance, demanded six on the ground that his adversary did not know the bunkers, and so would not be afraid of them. This claim, however, was rightly regarded as excessive.

SOME COURSES IN PARTICULAR.

Despite the weighty opinion quoted at the beginning of this chapter most golfers are amused by playing on new courses. Indeed there is hardly a pleasanter golfing holiday than that which consists of a voyage of discovery to a series of courses all fresh and all good. It would almost be worth while beginning golf all over again to enjoy it once more to the full.

Everybody remembers, or at any rate ought to remember, the delightful voyage of discovery through the golf courses of England made by Mr. Hutchinson, in his guise of the " Golfing Pilgrim " with his friend Mr. James Macpherson, the latter being a mythical gentleman, " pawkie " as to his play and Scottish as to his descent, whose game was " characterized by an unerring steadiness and unambitious length of drive, combined with a putting style of great deadliness." In re-reading the account of it there is a temptation to quote with an enhanced joy the episodes of the dead and derelict dog on the Bembridge beach and the long hole at Blackheath that made Mr. Macpherson feel as if he had been driving ever since he was a little boy. This has to be sternly resisted, but it is permissible to go through the pilgrimage once again, because it was made to ten courses that might be regarded as the representative English courses at that time, and so one can see at a glance how much golf and golf courses have changed and advanced. The precise date of this imaginary pilgrimage is rather difficult to ascertain, but it may perhaps be attributed for purposes of comparison to the early nineties.

The two pilgrims began at Hoylake ; then, leaving unvisited the other courses of Cheshire and Lancashire, made the formidable journey to Westward Ho ! Thence they went to Bembridge and thence, again turning inland, visited London and played at Wimbledon and Blackheath. After that came Sandwich, followed by no fewer than three East Anglian courses, Felixstowe, Yarmouth, and Brancaster. Finally the last short put was turned by the last blade of grass and the whole long-drawn-out match was halved at Alnmouth in Northumberland. It is rather interesting, if it be not irreverent, to consider how many of these courses would keep their places in an itinerary of to-day, presuming that the travellers, while not wholly without respect for antiquity, were yet chiefly moved by a desire to play good golf rather than merely to tee their balls upon historic ground. Nobody at least could complain of Hoylake as a starting place, for the glory of that admirable course has if anything increased with time. Mr. Macpherson might not like it so well, perhaps, since there are many more bunkers than of yore and he would not be able to "trundle his ball in ignominious security along the centre of the course" quite so easily.

Truly Hoylake is magnificent golf and there are some of the best and most exacting shots in the whole world to be played there, more especially when the north-west wind is blowing as fiercely as it did on the writer's last visit. The occasion was that of a tournament in which all the best professionals were playing and they assuredly did not make Hoylake look easy. There were two shots that fell to be played worthy of particular mention—the tee shot to "the Cop," which is the 4th hole, and the second shot to "the Briars," which is the 6th. There is nothing in the least remarkable in the appearance of "the Cop"; it is superficially a one-shot hole of moderate length, having a cross-bunker in front of the green, one cr two pot-bunkers on the right-hand edge of the green, and nothing particular beyond it. Nevertheless, when the hole is cut, as it was during this tournament, on the right-hand side of the green and the wind blows strongly from right to left, there is a stroke to be played so difficult that in both rounds of the final match it entirely defeated both parties. Unless the ball be held most resolutely right into the wind it is swept away round to the left and bounds 30, 40, or even 50 yards over the green ; yet if the ball is held up in the least degree too much, if there is more than a suspicion of slice on it, it is trapped either in the cross-bunker or the pot-bunkers as sure as fate. In fact " the Cop " is one of those holes—and there are much fewer than some people think—where mere straight, true hitting is hardly enough ; a real stroke of intense difficulty has to be played.

The second shot at " the Briars " is just such another ; the ball that is in the least hooked will career away for ever and there is a greedy clump of rushes just to the right of the flag to catch the one that is held up ever so little too much. In the first round of the final match, when the wind was at its fiercest, Braid and Duncan had both to attempt this shot ; each tackled it in his own characteristic way, but both were unsuccessful. Braid took · some form of iron club and tried to play one of his low forcing shots into the wind's eye, but there was much too much hook on the ball and the wind swept it far away to the left of the hole. Duncan took a wooden club and played a high shot with slice on it, a stroke at which he is wonderfully skilful. The slice was there, but there was too much of it, and the ball towered rather feebly against the wind and then fell to earth very short and many yards to

the right. As at " the Cop " the stroke was
just too difficult even for the very best of players.

To return after this digression to the pilgrim
and his itinerary, he could scarcely be allowed
to leave Liverpool without visiting another of
the many fine courses that surround it, for pre-
ference either Formby or Wallasey. Probably
it would be Formby, a good course of fine turf
and big menacing hills, so good that some people
think—although herein they are wrong—that it
is better than Hoylake. If Wales, and more
particularly Harlech, be out of the question,
Westward Ho ! would still come geographically
next, and, although some of its lovers might put
in a claim for Burnham with its cheerful carries
and towering mountains, the North Devon course
would still be the only one in the West. And
what a wonderful course it now is ! in the opinion
of most of those who played there in the Amateur
Championship of 1912 the very best in the whole
world of golf. Nowhere else perhaps is there to be
found the same combination of difficult and test-
ing holes with the inimitable splendour of natural
golfing country. Now comes the first unpleasant-
ness, for Bembridge, fascinating as it is and
having many devoted admirers, would have to
go, squeezed out by the long hitting of to-day,
and from Westward Ho ! the travellers could go
direct to London. In the courses of London is
the greatest change of all, for since the pilgrim's
puts " all ran bumpy," at Wimbledon a
whole race of new courses has sprung into
being, and sand, heather, and fir trees
have brought a new happiness into the drab
lives of London golfers. Wimbledon must
be expunged from the list without a moment's
hesitation, and not even its antiquity and
associations can save Blackheath. Out they

must both go, but it is almost too invidious to suggest two courses to supersede them. Sunningdale and Walton Heath are the two most obvious names, but then there is Swinley Forest, which is, one is disposed to think, for difficulty and amusement combined, the best of all inland courses. Moreover, if the pilgrim who is described as " a Jehu in driving " as compared with his opponent is to reap the reward of his hitting powers at Walton or Swinley, Mr. Macpherson might surely be entitled to insist on a day at Woking or Coombe Hill, where he might gain by avoiding bunkers placed diabolically near the hole or by rising superior to terrifying undulations in the greens.

Sandwich would again come next ; not the Sandwich of the original pilgrimage, but a much altered and, as the writer ventures to assert, a vastly improved one. Sandwich in one sense can hardly be improved, because it has an imperishable charm of its own which it is difficult either to heighten or impair. However rigorously the course is criticized—and it has in the past been subjected to much unsparing comment —the golfer in the street continues to enjoy the golf there, snaps his fingers ostentatiously in the critic's face, and is inclined to resent any proposed change as smacking of priggishness. Moreover he is entitled genuinely to lament the old Maiden, not the hole of a year or two back, but the original hole, for which one teed right under the highest part of the frowning, black-timbered mountain. However, that ancient tee has long since been rendered perilous by the rubber-cored ball and, apart from the Maiden, the alterations, while undoubtedly making the course a far finer test of golf, have not made it one whit less delightful or amusing save for those who are conservative to the degree of obstinacy or else cherish a misguided passion for blind strokes.

Sandwich once stood alone among the links of the South coast, but to choose only a single course in Kent would never do to-day. How would it be possible to overlook Deal, which is likewise a championship course, or Prince's, which is, on a windy day at least, more exacting even than either of its neighbours ? Moreover, when once upon that coast it would be a positive crime not to cross the Sussex border and visit one of the best of all courses at Rye. It is recorded that in the original matches Mr. Macpherson triumphed at Sandwich by following the blue flags in an unenterprising manner, but the blue flags, those props of the timid and the obese, have long since vanished from Sandwich, and one is disposed to think that James would to-day criticize it with " Oh aye, a fine green for a great slashing driver." Rye, with its road meandering through the heart of the course and its plentiful out of bounds, he would consider " a verra fine test of the real game of gowf."

Thus already there are nine courses in the list and room for only one more. Alnmouth must clearly share the fate of that other attractive nine-hole course, Bembridge, and the allowance of the Eastern Counties must be ruthlessly cut down. Yarmouth, pleasant as it is, must go, since in its present shape it is not long enough, and with much doubt and infinite regret we must rule out Felixstowe with it. Yet if the other holes at Felixstowe were like the 8th and 9th—Bunker's Hill and the Point—there would scarcely be a golf course in the world that could be compared with it.

SOME COURSES IN PARTICULAR.

Brancaster may be allowed to remain and make the tenth, although the mingled glories and terrors of the course have never been quite the same since the rubber-cored ball brought the once thrilling carries within the reach of the humblest. It seems hard that the journey cannot be extended rather further north, so as to include a short expedition inland as far as Ganton, but the number is now complete for better or worse. Only four of the original ten survive, but these things are only matters of opinion, and gross injustice may have been done to the other six. James Macpherson would almost certainly think so, for he would be sadly out-driven on some of the new courses.

Ten is, of course, too small a number nowadays, for there are, one might almost say, hundreds of courses that repay the trouble of visiting them. It is instructive to read, although it would be impolitic to mention the names of some of the courses that were seriously considered before the historic pilgrimage, although not actually visited. On some of them a golfer would now scarcely dream of playing unless he was compelled to, and it is this that gives one perhaps the clearest insight into the wonderful increase of good courses in England.

There is one course that had perforce to be left out of the chosen ten, to which nevertheless any pilgrim should make a separate and particular expedition, and if he have in him a right measure of reverence, it will be with a most genuine thrill of pleasure that he comes to the first home of golf in England, " the bleak and sandy ridges of Blackheath." In the clubhouse he will find an ancient tradition upheld with all becoming pride and in the golf itself much to interest, to please and to try him.

It may not perhaps quite coincide with his preconceived notions of good golf, since golfers have come to expect as a matter of right that one or two rules should be observed by those who lay out courses for them. If, for example, they hit the ball to the exact spot which expert local opinion points out as the right one, they insist on finding it lying remarkably well upon grass. Further, should there be a hazard between the green and the ball, thus perfectly struck, they demand that it should, however difficult, be actually possible to pitch the ball over the bunker in such a way that it will stop on the green. A course laid out on principles of anarchy, where the ideally-hit ball may rest in a thick tussock of grass or on a gravelly patch perfectly void of grass, and where, moreover, the player is seriously advised to pitch his ball either short of the hazard or actually in it with the openly avowed intention of playing for the bounce, would strike the modern golfer as no less improper than bewildering. No doubt he would be quite right, and no doubt also the almost diabolic skill of the golfing " architect " makes for the greater happiness as well as for the greater moral good of his victims. Nevertheless, it is sometimes most delightful and refreshing to slink shamefacedly away from the courses laid out with the nicest judgment of gigantic intellects and indulge in a day's low dissipation : to attack holes that represent no particular multiple of no particular shot and hazards for which there is no architect but Nature to abuse, the only consideration being that they happen to be in the way and must somehow be circumvented.

SOME COURSES IN PARTICULAR.

Two holes may be quoted as instances of golf
as Nature made it. One is the 2nd hole, which
used to be the 1st until the Royal Blackheath
Club moved to their present very charming
house on the edge of the heath. The hole lies
perched on a small plateau on the far side of a
pit, and it can be reached with a single shot
from the tee. There is a slightly following
wind, and the ground is as hard as iron ; so
the player—wisely, as he thinks—takes an
iron club, lofted in some degree, and hits the
ball as hard, as high, and as straight as he can.
The shot appears a perfect one ; the ball alights
just over the pit and close to the hole—clears
with one frenzied leap the railings beyond the
green, and is last seen bounding playfully away
down a hard, high road in the direction of some
neighbouring suburb. Yet, let it not be
hastily thought that this is not a good as well
as an entertaining hole, nor that a good shot
cannot be played at it, for the skilful player
well advised will pitch his ball on a particular
place at the foot of the rise, whence the ball
will bound, not on to the road, but on to the
green.

At the 4th hole again a road runs close in
front of the green, and no human skill will
make the ball pitch over it and stop upon the
green. But there is a stroke of real skill to
be played by which the ball will pitch just
short of the road and so bound thence on to
and not over the green, a shot requiring not
only courage but an ability, possessed by the
professional and lacking in most amateurs, of
pitching a ball with a mashie, not within an
area, but on a definite spot. The road is there
and the green is there and, all preconceived
notions of fairness and unfairness having been

with difficulty expelled from the mind, it is wonderful what can be done and how extremely interesting it is to try to do it—far more interesting than many a cut-and-dried shot upon a shaven lawn.

Nowhere is the true glory of the rule which demands that the ball should be played where it lies better illustrated. The spectacle of a gentleman in an old and weather-beaten red coat waiting patiently on a road for the leisurely passage of a milkcart before attempting to dislodge the ball from under the edge of a footpath is one that puts the stranger to shame when he thinks of the number of times he has lifted and dropped under an inadequate penalty upon other courses. He feels that he has lived hitherto in cottonwool and is now for the first time confronted by the stern realities of golfing life. It is indeed sad that one of the many roads at Blackheath now possesses a camber so steep and an edge of stonework so uncompromising and precipitous that one exception to the universal rule has perforce been made.

The charm of the Blackheath hazards is that they are natural, although the term must be used in a rather peculiar sense, signifying an obstacle planted there, not by nature, but by entirely non-golfing man. The roads are there primarily to walk upon, the seats to sit upon, and as the passers-by do sit on them in large numbers it is somewhat alarming to be given the line as midway between two seats. Yet one of these unorthodox hazards, cunningly placed, can make a wonderfully interesting approach shot out of one that would otherwise be featureless. Just one short length of iron railings at the right-hand side of the 6th green really governs the play throughout that exceedingly long hole by compelling the player to keep to the left if he desires a reasonably easy approach shot. Just that projecting angle of the wall round the club-house garden demands the most skilful of hooks if the last green is to be reached from the tee.

To deal with such unflinching hazards as walls and roads and railings demands, of course, a frame of mind carefully cultivated for the occasion. So in some measure does the playing of quite short and open approaches, for, as was once written of the High hole at St. Andrews—

> The green is small, and broken is the ground
> Which doth that little charmed space surround.

The playing of little running-up shots from the borders of the green demands not only a delicate touch but a confidence amounting to positive arrogance. It may well be that the stranger will allow himself at times to become exasperated at his own bad luck or the outrageous good fortune of his opponent, but, even in his most irritable moments, he appreciates the fact that the course is one to repay good golf in the end. Its abiding charm, however, lies not in the precise merits of any hole or shot over which there may well be disputes, but in its purely natural and primitive character. It is the Windmill Down or Broad Halfpenny of golf, and as such to be played in a becoming spirit, with a reverent and yet with a light heart.

III.

PROFESSIONAL AND AMATEUR.

One of the invariable results of watching an Open Championship is to leave the spectator wondering in a moody and despairing manner as to the superiority of the professional over the amateur. The reason why the professional plays better is by no means hard to discover; he plays more and he is paid to do it. Wherein precisely the superiority lies it is not so easy to see. The first and most obvious answer, that the professional is better at every part of the game, is not quite true, because, although the bad putting of good players is always liable to be exaggerated, the most eminent professionals do sometimes really put so badly that it is almost inconceivable that any one should put worse. Another possible answer to the question, and that which is perhaps most frequently given, is that the superiority lies chiefly in the long iron shots up to the hole. This would be an excellent answer if the best professionals had to play long iron shots rather more often, but the chief impression left on the mind after having watched them play on a still day is that, however long the course, their second shots are as a rule played with a goose-necked niblick. In short, it is the extraordinary and consistent length of the tee shots that makes the best professionals' game so unassailably good.

Most of those amateurs who have something

of a reputation for long driving have their good days and their bad days; not only are they not always straight, but they are by no means always long. Their length is like Mr. Bob Acres's courage: it "will come and go," whereas the professionals' length is persistent and remorseless. It is accompanied, too, by an accuracy which can perhaps best be gauged by the feelings of the onlookers. For example, to take a wooden club from the third tee at Muirfield necessitates a shot through an excessively narrow opening between a bunker on the right and a swamp on the left—so narrow that most self-respecting amateurs would certainly play short with an iron club. In the Championship of 1912 the professionals, with the exception of Massy, who was always cautious, took their drivers and lashed out manfully with them. Yet one never watched this shot with any particular anxiety or interest: one knew where the ball would be at the end of the stroke— exactly midway between the bunker and the swamp—and there it almost invariably was. As to a topped tee shot, the possibility of such a thing never entered into one's head, and the tee shot over the big hill at the 6th was not in the least more thrilling to watch than any other in the case of any of the good players.

In a large degree, no doubt, the professionals hit so very far because they hit so very straight; both virtues proceed from the same cause, extreme cleanness of hitting and accuracy of timing, which through much practice have become a second nature. But apart from this they seem to owe something of their length to the fact that they have more and more developed the art of hitting, as opposed to the older one of sweeping or swinging. One and all, they appear to give the ball what can best be described as a terrific punch, and the follow through plays but a very secondary part in the proceedings. True, the club comes through with the impetus of the hit, but the effective part of the stroke is really over by that time; the follow through never seems to be of such importance as the beginner is taught in the text-books (and probably very wisely taught) to regard it. For example, there is hardly one among the professionals who plays even in the very least degree after the manner of Mr. John Ball. It is not merely that Mr. Ball's style is inimitable; it is a radical difference of method between one who relies chiefly on the swing of the club and the other who hits. That hitting is the order of the day is, of course, no new discovery, but it becomes more apparent every year, and every year the professionals seem to drive better and better.

The ordinary amateur who watches Ray playing so-called "two-shot" holes with a drive and a niblick is apt to say, "If I only had him to drive for me, I could do all the holes in 4, too." This is, of course, a harmless and amiable delusion, because he could really do nothing of the sort. What he could do would be to reach the confines of the green and then (on the tortuous Muirfield greens, at any rate) take his three puts. He could not, whatever he may think, lay the ball nearly so close to the hole, even with a niblick, as the professional, whose quite short pitch is almost as impressive in its accuracy as the full drive. It is played for one thing with such a wonderful and enviable confidence; the club is taken so well and freely away; the ball is struck so hard. Any one who has ever seen Taylor giving an indoor exposition of how a mashie shot should be played knows how the boards rattle and the clouds of dust ascend from the carpet beneath those tremendous thuds.

An unworthy suspicion sometimes comes into one's mind as to the reason of the amateur's passionate appreciation of the side bunker; he is never quite certain that he is not going to "fluff" a pitching shot, and so prefers nothing in his way. The professional, on the other hand, is perfectly certain that he is going to do nothing of the sort, wherefore he may sometimes think a cross-hazard even a better one than it is. He certainly can hit the ball with his mashie with astonishing precision, and nowhere is this better seen than when his ball lies clean in a bunker. Even in the most critical moments, moments which might make him put as nervously and badly as the heart of the amateur could desire, he may be trusted not to take even a teaspoonful too much sand. It is a gift that makes the golfer take risks with a light heart and so take them successfully.

This extraordinary and sustained excellence of modern professional golf has completely upset all the old ideas of score play. Time was when match play was supposed to be for the dashing and brilliant, score play for the steady and humdrum. In the ordinary club competition this theory often holds good to-day, and the man who jogs along, keeping a level head and an untorn card and avoiding a preponderance of sevens and eights, will sometimes astonish himself and other people by proving to be the winner. With the best players it is a different matter; a match may possibly be the occasion for watching and waiting and playing short when the disasters of a single adversary afford a short breathing space. In score play there is no breathing space, no relaxation of pressure, and golf is indeed what Mr. Low has declared that it ought always to be—" a contest of risks."

Nothing is more noticeable in the Open Championship than the big risks that the players are constantly taking, and taking as a rule with success. To turn for a moment to an older championship, that at Sandwich in 1911, one shot may be quoted which especially impressed itself upon the memory. Going to the 13th hole Taylor hooked his drive, and his ball lay among the hills to the left ; the grass was by no means short, the stance mountainous and difficult, and the distance to the bunker in front of the green decidedly long, even had the ball been teed. Yet Taylor did not seem to hesitate, but instantly attacked the shot with some wooden club ; what is more, he hit it so well that but for a trifle of pull he would have carried safely on to the green ; as it was, the ball was just caught in the far left-hand end of the bunker. This stroke appeared, to the writer at least, a remarkable instance of the high pressure that must be kept up by those who aspire to win Open Championships. Another among many good examples of the same thing was to be found in the second hole at Sandwich. Here the wind blew strongly behind the players so that a cleanly hit ball could easily reach the bunkers that guard the green and are only very slightly to the right of the exact bee-line from tee to flag. To the left there are more bunkers, to say nothing of the knotted horrors of exceedingly long grass, and the only way of safety is a very narrow hog's back of turf from which the ball may, and often does, kick either to right or left. Nevertheless, hardly any one seemed to consider the policy of playing short of the right-hand bunkers with a cleek or spoon ; with the very remote chance of hitting a drive very long, very straight, and very lucky along the hog's back they all went hammer and tongs for the green, and generally ended their career in the bunker. Yet so skilful was the bunker play that the hole was generally done in four : another illustration of the fact that a genuine confidence in oneself and one's niblick is a great aid to courage.

It has already been said that the best of professionals do occasionally put quite surprisingly ill, and these lapses are of course the more noticeable because of the contrast with the almost uniform perfection of their play up to the green. The spectator takes all the other strokes as a matter of course and in describing the play harps only on the short puts that were missed.

Thus perhaps the chief impression left on the spectator's mind after watching all the most distinguished professionals play for three days over Hoylake in the spring of 1912 was that of the really absurd difficulty of putting. It is by no means an original one, and yet every now and again it thrusts itself forward with all the force of a revelation. The Hoylake greens were very slow, and so long as the ball was firmly hit very true ; the players were the best that exist, and yet there was remarkably little good putting to be seen, and a great deal that was very bad. A perfect epidemic of shortness seized on nearly all the competitors ; even the usually blameless Sherlock would often leave the ball 4ft. short of the hole, and it might be said of Braid, as was once said of old Tom Morris, that he would have been a good putter " gin the hole was aye a yaird nearer till him."

It might be inferred from these remarks that other and less distinguished people would have putted better than the professionals, but it is most improbable that they would have done anything of the sort. Many bad golfers cherish the belief that they can put better than the champions, but it is a delusion as complete as it is singular, whereof the fallacy lies, not in thinking that good golfers put badly, but in failing to notice that bad golfers put much worse. Yet knowing this and having years of painful experience of the impossibilty of putting, one still continues to wonder how those who are so faultless in all other strokes can be so often and so entirely futile in this one. It might be imagined that a person who spends most of his life with a golf club in hand ought to be able to devise some system whereby at a range of 6ft. on a good green he could hit the edge of the hole even if he did not steer the ball into it ; but this is clearly not so, since more often than not he does neither the one nor the other. The fact presumably is that we can all appreciate our own difficulties in putting, but not those of any one else.

In watching the professionals put there is one thing that strikes the spectator very constantly, and that is that the fact that they began the game as very small boys is of far less service to them on the greens than anywhere else. It may even have been an actual disadvantage. For some reason the small caddie naturally acquires a beautifully free and correct style in driving and iron play, but his style of putting, as may be seen any day in the neighbourhood of the caddies' shed, has little to recommend it. It consists of a jerky, stabbing stroke, played more often than not with a mashie, the only club the boy has got, and this stroke is apt to survive when he has come to man's estate and has the choice of all the putters in his own shop. There are, of course, many very fine putters amongst the professionals—no doubt they put on the average better than does any one else—but the typical professional style of putting is not nearly so good as is their style in playing all other strokes. One can hardly conceive their method of driving being improved upon ; it is so obviously sound as well as graceful, but it is quite another matter on the green. Players who hit the ball with the perfect smoothness and trueness of Tom Ball or Sherlock stand out conspicuously from among their fellows.

We are rather apt to talk in a vague and general way as if there was but one professional or professionally-modelled style in playing golf, and it is certainly rare, except among the artisan golfers of Scotland, to see an amateur that one could possibly mistake for a professional. Even before he begins to hit the ball the professional has a method of making a tee, born perhaps of early years of carrying clubs, that the amateur cannot imitate. The amateur clumsily and slowly takes the ball in one hand and the sand in the other, whereas the professional, with the air of a conjuror producing an unexpected bowl of gold fish, makes his tee and puts the ball upon it, all apparently with one hand and all in a moment. Yet, when it comes to hitting the ball, there is really an infinite variety of styles among the professionals. Let us by way of example take a look at a meeting at which most of the good players of the younger school are present ; it is in fact the foursome tournament of the southern section of the Professional Golfers' Association which was played a year or so since at Fulwell. In our search for the true orthodoxy we shall soon have our brains in a whirl of conflicting images. Here for instance is Tom Ball, about as fine a golfer as there is in the field. Ball outrages nearly all the proprieties, or at any rate the earnest student's preconceived notions of them. In one respect he has lately made a step towards orthodoxy, since he no longer moves his left foot in the middle of his swing. He has a very odd knuckling motion of the right leg and seems to pirouette lightly on the left toe; the toe still evidently wants to move its position, but, after a struggle with its conscience, as it were, it just succeeds in remaining steady. His method of swinging the club is, however, a very remarkable one. One of the first lessons that the learner has been taught, and rightly taught, is that as the club goes up so it will come down, but Ball's club seems to despise so monotonous a routine; for, unless there be some optical illusion in the matter, it goes up by one road and comes down by quite another. On the way up he appears to take the club well in to himself and round his legs, but he brings it down much further away from his body, so that it describes a kind of loop. This peculiarity is more particularly noticeable in his iron shots, but it may also be seen in his play with wooden clubs and there is even a trace of it in his putting. Anybody else who should adopt this style would presumably hit a series of horrible slices, varied by an occasional shot in which he would smother the ball and send it towards short-leg. It is a most baffling eccentricity of genius, for Ball is not only an admirably accurate hitter, but, for one of his slight physique, a wonderfully long one.

PROFESSIONAL AND AMATEUR.

His partner, Robson, a most graceful as well as a most powerful player, comes much nearer to the ideal, although his very full long swing may be regarded nowadays as something of an anachronism. As to the other two players in the final round, there is nothing very noticeable about Kettley, who has a neat, compact style rather lacking in hitting power, but his partner, Johns, goes through a series of very singular movements. Almost alone among good players he has his left elbow in the up swing not close to his body but sticking out at the most awkward angle, while he deliberately turns his head away from the ball, as if to help the turn of the body. He seems to come back to the ball in a curious sideways attitude, which, according to all the wisdom of the ancients, should produce a slice ; yet he hits the ball exceedingly straight, and is, moreover, constantly surprising one by his length.

Turning to some of the other players, there is further variety to be observed. Duncan has, of course, a beautiful swing, although its tremendous speed, combined with its upright character, would probably bring down disaster upon the head of many of his imitators. The style of his partner, Mayo, on the other hand, is *sui generis* among those of professional golfers. Any one who for the first time saw Mayo swing a club, without taking into account the length and accuracy of his shot, might think that he was a studious amateur who had learnt the game with much labour from golfing text-books. There is no one who so palpably conforms to the well-worn doctrine of the turning over of the left wrist. He seems to be turning over that wrist for ever and ever, and there is also a very marked turning movement of the whole body and a slightly less noticeable turn of the head. Nevertheless Mayo straightens out the tangle in a wonderful way in the down swing, and his finish, when he is in his best form, comes near to the *beau idéal* of orthodoxy. The very elaborate turning movement is possibly due to the fact that Mayo is practically unique among fine players, in that the knuckles of his left hand do not point heavenward. He holds his left hand pronouncedly under the club, and a player who holds the club thus, and still gets it to the stereotyped position at the top of the swing, must necessarily do a great deal of turning, as any one can discover for himself by experiment. To instance one more variety of style, Hepburn, a very good golfer indeed, has comparatively little turn of his body or of the left foot, but takes the club up noticeably high over his head and mainly with his arms. He consequently has a very firm-footed finish, a little, perhaps, like that of Taylor, although there is absolutely no other similarity between their styles.

It would be rather interesting to hear the opinion of some old golfer as to whether there really is a greater diversity of styles among the professionals than there was 30 or even 20 years ago. It may exist only in the individual observer's imagination. On the other hand, there are now a far larger number of professionals than there used to be, and, which is still more to the point, they have learned in a far larger number of schools. Time was when the distinguished professionals might almost be divided into the St. Andrews school and the Musselburgh school, although one must not forget Elie, that produced the Simpsons, Douglas Rolland, and Braid; and doubtless a Scottish historian could mention other exceptions. Since then have sprung up in England the schools of Westward Ho! Hoylake, and Jersey, and there are, moreover, hundreds of English professionals who have picked up the game more or less for themselves on courses scattered all over the country. It would hardly be surprising, therefore, if there should have been discovered more different ways of arriving at the same accurate result.

IV.

PRACTICE AND THEORY.

It is in the spring, with the lengthening of the days beyond the time of the second round, that the golfer's fancy turns to thoughts of practising, more especially after tea. There are three distinct motives which may actuate him. First, he may practise because he has nothing else to do and likes to be in the open air, in which case he may do much good to himself but little to his golf; secondly he may wish to improve his mind by learning a new stroke, and this may be highly beneficial so long as he does not fall a victim to that pernicious form of lunacy which dictates the playing of a complicated stroke when a straightforward one will do much better; thirdly—and this is the commonest and most depressing case—he may go out with the ambition, not of improving his play, but of preventing it from becoming worse—in short, because he is in a more or less chronic condition of being " off it " with some particular club.

The practiser of this last type may be subdivided into two very different persons. The unimaginative player will take out a caddie to pick up the balls and will thump away doggedly with the recalcitrant club for a certain definite number of strokes. If he hits no more successfully than he did in his round, he will not greatly mind nor be tempted beyond the number of strokes originally prescribed; if he hits better he will neither know the reason of it nor will he inquire, but will wisely rest content with the mere fact of his improvement.

The practiser of imaginative and poetical temperament, which is the worst of all possible temperaments for golf, will proceed on quite different lines. He will take no caddie with him, since the delicate experiments that he proposes to himself must be conducted in the most complete privacy; neither will he prescribe for his cure any definite length of time, since everything must depend upon how many entirely different styles he will be compelled to try. The practiser of this turn of mind may, of course, rise to heights of ecstasy which are quite unknown to the less emotional; he has not only the intellectual satisfaction of having thought out his own cure, but, if he stops at the right moment, he enjoys for the rest of the evening the touching belief that he will never play badly again.

On the other hand there are terrible pitfalls which beset his path, and of these the most serious is that of trying more than a limited number of styles. It may be safely laid down that if a player has in the space of a quarter of an hour made three separate and important discoveries as to style, all of which prove perfectly futile in the matter of causing the ball to fly, he will be very ill-advised if he try to make a fourth. It is abundantly clear that no one thing but rather everything is the matter, and that there is nothing for it but stolid and prayerful thumping. Yet this is one of the most agonizing acts of renunciation that can be asked from the genuine practiser. He cannot bear to go in with nothing to look forward to on the morrow but a round for which he has no theory ready. A circumstance which often makes it the more bitter is that by some curious fatality it always becomes too dark to play any more at precisely the moment when he was just about to think of the right remedy.

The spring then is not necessarily a season of unmixed happiness for the golfer; it brings with it some disappointments as well as many pleasures. The pleasures are easily enumerated —the basking in the sun, the sitting on the grass, the discarding of woolly waistcoats—they are really too obvious to mention. The disappointing part of the affair is to discover that which one has often discovered before but lightheartedly forgotten, that continuous instead of occasional golf does not always mean improvement. Indeed, it too often happens that the Easter holiday-maker, after playing reasonably well on the Friday, deteriorates steadily until the Monday evening, when he returns home a tired and embittered man.

The fact is that the golfer, like the runner, has to get his "second wind," and an Easter holiday is often not quite long enough for the purpose. At the end of a week he would very possibly be at his best, but at the end of four days he is as likely as not to be suffering from an early attack of staleness, more especially if he has started recklessly and joyfully upon a course of three rounds a day. The best that can be said for the three-round habit is that, if the holiday be short and the weather seraphic, the pleasure may be worth the consequences. From a serious, doubtless too serious, point of view it is wholly to be deprecated. There are a few golfers who apparently cannot play too much, but go from strength to strength. They are usually possessed of qualities that go some way towards the making of champions—great physical strength, an invincible keenness, and, perhaps best of all, a lack of imagination. The imaginative golfer, if he be playing well, thinks that this happy state of things cannot go on for ever ; he grows frightened of his own good strokes and goes to meet trouble halfway. His unimaginative brother, if he thinks at all, thinks merely that he is playing well and leaves the future to look after itself.

At the end of these first few days of continuous golf the great mass of players will declare, and that only too truthfully, that their play has been infamous. Of the rest, some will say that they have played well, and others that they are playing well ; and it is to be observed that between these two statements there is more than a verbal difference. The first implies a thankfulness for unexpected mercies and a grave doubt as to their continuance ; the man who " has played well " may play vilely next week. But he who " is playing well " will not play badly next week, nor in all probability the week after ; he is not cringingly grateful to Providence, but confident in himself. He is so confident that he does not in the least mind if he makes a bad stroke, and the way in which a golfer regards a bad stroke affords an admirable index to the game that he is playing. If he be in the lowest depths of despair he regards the first bad stroke of the day as the beginning of the end ; if in a state of moderately low spirits, he thinks it a rather disquieting circumstance, the causes of which merit careful investigation ; if in a confident and proper state of mind, he dismisses it as a pure accident—a thing that happened for no particular reason, and will not happen again. This last and wholly desirable frame of mind is very rare in the early summer but comparatively common in September when the last golden sands of the holidays are just running out and many golfers have spent three blissful weeks or so in the open air doing little else but playing golf. They are all in the condition of " never having played so well in their lives," but, though they do not know it—the end of last year's holiday being buried in a merciful oblivion—this happy state will more or less shortly and quite certainly be exchanged for that of " not being able to hit a shot. " This miserable consummation is not always arrived at immediately. With some the beneficial results of a reasonably strenuous golfing holiday abide for a considerable time ; they continue to play well for some while after returning home, and their own courses appear wonderfully and beautifully easy as compared with those they have left. With others the crash is apt to come at once ; a period of continuous golf followed by a week's abstinence makes the club feel as unwieldy in the hand as a cricket bat, the whole game hopelessly strange and difficult, and they have to play through a period of utter despair, lucky if they ultimately win through to a St. Martin's summer, in which some traces of their holiday confidence return to them. It is to be presumed that the first of these two classes is the more fortunate, and yet that is by no means certain, for the delusion that one has made a permanent improvement may by lasting the longer bring in the end the more bitter disappointment.

The first and rudest shock that awaits the homing golfer is the discovery that driving is not nearly so easy a matter as he thought it.

PRACTICE AND THEORY.

Driving may be said to be the most mechanical part of golf, and when the machinery is being used every day it ought to and generally does work with reasonable smoothness, but it is apt to resent rust and disuse by becoming most sadly out of gear. The man playing golf every day is less likely to break down seriously in his driving than in anything else, but winter, when it has once set in, may be one long break-down, so that he pulls and slices amongst the heather and the fir trees for one weary week-end after another. The player who is gifted with a steady, easy style of driving, who keeps his body still and does not pirouette over much upon his toes, is likely to reap his richest harvest of half-crowns during these winter months ; for lack of practice will not affect him so adversely as his more florid and vehement brother, who can perhaps drive steadily enough when he has got his eye in and has no time to get it out again.

The case of putting is different from that of driving. For one thing putting is so subtle an art that no man's putting can become mechanical, practise he never so wisely, and so regular play or the lack of it is the less likely to affect him. Indeed, it is at least arguable that the golfer is likely to put better when he plays only at week-ends and not throughout all the week. A great many people do their putting on the principle attributed to Mr. A. F. Macfie, although their results are not as a rule by any means so satisfactory as his ; it is that of putting on a different system every day. Since Mr. Macfie, as far as is humanly possible, never puts badly, his power of inventing new systems must be almost infinite, but other people are less gifted ; when one system breaks down and there is no good one to take its place they put badly, and go on putting badly till their inventive genius has recuperated. Now when one or at most only two days in the week have to be provided for, it is possible to devise a sufficient number of systems to tide the winter successfully over; the inventor has the other five days in the week and the dining-room carpet at his disposal, and his powers are not unduly strained. Against this must be set the loss of an instinctive sense of the strength which comes from playing day after day on the same greens, but the most appalling putting break-down consists not so much in an inability to lay the ball dead as to hole it out when it is dead. That is beyond question the nethermost hell.

In the case of the ordinary golfer who is neither better nor worse than his fellows it is not the driver nor the putter that will betray him most grievously when he is out of practice: it is the brassey that is the arch-traitor. When he was playing every day he was as steady with a wooden club through the green as he was from the tee, but in winter there is a different tale to tell, and this is the more exasperating because in winter courses are at their longest and "two-shot holes" almost worthy of their name.

To be sure the lies through the green on many an inland course in winter are often so bad as to make brassey play very difficult even for a skilful player. Nay, they are not bad lies at all in the nobler sense of the words, the sense in which they are used by those who lament the too great perfection of modern green-keeping. To nip the ball out of a sandy cup, to flick it cleanly as it lies close on bare and iron-hard turf, to tear it away from an ancient divot-mark, even while cursing the hand that failed

to replace the turf—in such deeds as these there
is a genuine and pleasurable thrill, and at the
worst failure is not wholly inglorious. But
continually to plunge the head of the brassey
into oozy clay so that it emerges black, horrible,
and bespattered with worm-casts—this is only
to humiliate and degrade a faithful servant.
It is better that the brassey should repose,
neglected in the bag, than be put to such usage.
All courses, however, are not quagmires and on
the most playable the man who is master of his
wooden club through the green may reap a rich
reward during the winter months. There will
always, needless to say, be considerable difference of opinion as to what constitutes a bad lie
for a wooden club, not only between the player
who bemoans it and his wholly unsympathetic
adversary, but also in circumstances render-
ing possible a more impartial judgment. Many
golfers, taught by a bitter experience, will
regard as only suitable to the lofting iron a lie
from which Vardon will nonchalantly hit the
ball, not with a brassey, but with a driver.
Those more especially who have come to the
game comparatively late in life and have a
rather stiff, short swing are often incapable
of picking the ball up through the green, although
they may be excellent drivers from the tee.
Curiously enough, it is often these very same
players who pride themselves upon their skill
with a spoon, a club which (more particularly
if it have some affectionate and diminutive
name, such as " Pug " or " Toby ") they are
apt to regard as an enchanter's wand. Into
the reason of the occult powers of this club
they apparently think it impious to pry further,
for if they do indeed use their intelligence in the
matter they do so to singularly little purpose.

If the shot to be played is, according to strictly orthodox opinions, a brassey shot, then a brassey it must be ; they either top the ball quite simply or else endeavour to hoist it upward by a curtseying movement of the knees and a ducking of the right shoulder, hoping apparently by this gesture of oriental politeness to induce it to rise. If, on the other hand, the distance from the hole is such that they can conscientiously use a spoon, they will hit the ball as cleanly and confidently as may be. But the tremendous feat of putting two and two together, of observing that the face of the spoon is much set back, while that of the brassey is nearly straight, and of drawing the right conclusion from these facts, is comparatively rare. If it were not, the file of the clubmaker would be kept busy during the winter months, brasseys would be more lofted, and impotent brassey players far less frequent than they are at present.

Meanwhile though the spoon is not always very wisely used by its owner it is the fashionable club of the hour. Writing some 20 years ago the learned author of the Badminton volume on Golf committed himself to the statement that " the modern golfer had reduced the complexity of his manifold spoons almost to the simplicity of a single brassey." To-day hardly any self-respecting golfer can array himself for battle without at least one spoon of some sort or other. Everybody has a club that he calls a spoon, but individual golfers' ideas of the chief characteristics of the club vary amazingly. As opposed to the old race of spoons—long, mid, and short—most of the modern ones have this in common, that they are shod with brass ; but there are spoons that are merely drivers very slightly grassed, such, for instance, as are used by Mr. Norman Hunter, who entirely eschews clubs having brass soles. Of the clubs which are lofted enough *primâ facie* to justify their title, there are some which are light and toylike and others that are formidable bludgeons, larger, heavier, and longer than the drivers used by a great many people ; as to these weapons it will generally be found that their owners allude to them as " my little baffy," either from affection or possibly with a desire to impress the hearers with the colossal distances to be compassed by a club of such a diminutive name if wielded by skilful hands.

Although clubs of such widely different types all go by the name of spoon, there is not any very startling difference in their owners' methods of wielding them. This is true of an enormous proportion of the great army of spoon-players, but there are, of course, some highly distinguished golfers with great reputations as wielders of this club who play with it special and distinctive strokes. Mr. Hilton's spoon is certainly the most famous of all spoons : yet its battered and venerable physiognomy is likely to be a little disappointing to those who have made a pilgrimage especially to see it ; at a first glance it looks like an old cut-down driver, which is, in fact, just what it happens to be. The results achieved with it, however, are certainly astonishing, whether it be the wonderfully dead fall of the ball upon the green or the owners complete mastery over the club in regard to distance, for Mr. Hilton will not infrequently play a spoon shot, where many a second-class amateur would consider himself disgraced if he took any club more powerful than an iron.

Duncan, again, is the master of a most beautiful and effective spoon shot, played with a good deal of cut. One particular instance comes to mind from a recent foursome tournament— a full spoon shot played up to the 17th hole at Walton Heath; it can be appreciated, of course, only by those who know this famous hole. The hole was cut close to the right-hand edge of the green, and so was but a few yards from the top of the precipitous bank; the ball, played rather from the left-hand side of the course, pitched well past the hole, yet stopped so quickly as not to plunge over the precipice. The shot was not in reality a perfect one, for it was clearly cut rather more than Duncan intended, but the amount of stop on the ball was, when one considers the length of the shot, quite extraordinary. Mr. Horace Hutchinson, too, having in his later years rather given up cleeks and driving irons, is a most accomplished wielder of the aluminium spoon, more especially out of the tenacious Ashdown heather, and Mr. John Low has a whole gradation of spoon shots at his command, including some wrist-shots that are quite *sui generis*. But in the hands of ordinary mortals the spoon is capable of none of these flights. They may talk learnedly of the shots that they have " cut up into a right-hand wind " with the magic club and of the wondrous dead fall on the green that ensued, but in fact these things only happen in the imagination, or, if the shot was ever successfully played, many and many a hole has since been lost by the attempt to repeat it. To the average golfer a spoon is just a lofted brassey and nothing more, and he would do well to pry no further into its mysteries.

Some very stern teachers would perhaps tell him to burn his spoon and learn to play his cleek and iron properly, but this would probably be a mistake, just as it is a mistake impetuously to turn several clubs out of the bag on the general ground that there are too many in it. This is a resolution the golfer is apt to make either after carrying his own bag of clubs for a very short distance or reading of some wonderful achievement with a single club, such as Ernest Foord's 73 with his putter at Burnham. Further, perhaps, he reflects on his last round and finds that unless he has had to ply the niblick with exceptional frequency, the vast majority of strokes have been played with four clubs—driver, iron, mashie, and putter.

Before, however, he acts on any hastily made resolutions and discards some half dozen, as he now deems them, superfluous clubs from his bag, he will do well to examine the sets of clubs belonging to the professionals. The professionals possess pre-eminently the gift of being able to do marvels with a single club; yet it will almost invariably be found that they carry as full a sheaf as any amateur. Several of their clubs they may use, if at all, only on a single occasion in the course of a match, but still they deem each one of them well worth the carrying.

The real point is probably this—that it is in learning the game rather than in playing it that there is much virtue in few clubs. The professional in the early days of his caddie-hood has an extremely small stock of clubs; he will be a lucky boy if he has more than one of his very own, and to possess three would make him something of a millionaire amongst his fellows. So, with necessity to drive him, he learns to play a variety of strokes with one and the same club. He learns that if his single iron will hit the ball too far with a full shot, he has just got to play a half-shot; that the ball must by some method or other be kept down against a wind and must be heavily cut if it is to pitch dead over a bunker. He and his club master these difficulties together and become part of one another in a way rarely to be found amongst amateurs. The amateur is apt to get over his early difficulties in a much simpler way. Instead of learning that shot which is most characteristic of the best professionals, the half-shot with the straight-faced iron, he extracts from an indulgent parent the price of a light iron, which he whirls round his head with the exuberantly full swing of boyhood. From the same source he obtains a liberally lofted mashie or niblick, with which he may indeed get the ball high and easily into the air, but he will not gain the mastery over the club as does the caddie. Golfing Waterloos are not won on the playing fields of Eton, but on the bare patch of ground beside the caddie shed.

V.

PRELIMINARY ADDRESSES.

It is one of the most depressing, as it is one of the most commonplace, of the truths which the golfer comes gradually to appreciate that to any other eye but his own mind's eye, his style always appears exactly the same. He will often find, when he imagines that he has revolutionized his methods beyond all recognition, that a tactless friend will in fact recognize him from the crest of a hill on the far horizon and will make the disillusionment the more bitter by remarking, " I should know your swing a mile off." On the other hand, it is only once in a decade, and then when he is himself unconscious of any change, that a sympathetic observer will say to him, " I say, you've altered your style, haven't you ? " Practically speaking, the only difference that our friends ever see in our play, save the obvious one between hitting and missing the ball, is that on one day our swing is reasonably smooth and harmonious and on another snatchy, hurried, and without rhythm.

Yet, if they are obtusely blind to those epoch-making changes in the actual swing, of which we ourselves are so acutely conscious, they can see certain things which are often hidden from us. When we are addressing the ball in a state of comparative repose, before becoming in the actual stroke a mere vision of whirling arms and legs, then our friends can, and do, see much better than we can ourselves whether we have departed from our normal stance. Every one of us must sometimes have been told that he is standing much more open or has the ball much further back than usual, and more often than not, having denied the charge with indignation and astonishment, he will have had ultimately to admit the truth of it. The prosaic onlooker who cannot follow our higher flights of fancy is not altogether without his usefulness.

A priori it would appear likely enough that we should vary a little from day to day in the comparatively complex act of swinging, but quite absurd that we should not be able to stereotype our simple preliminary attitude. As a fact, however, it is just in these preliminaries that we do constantly vary, very often while quite unaware of it ourselves. Certain of these unconscious variations are for some mysterious reason very much more common than others, and so must be the more carefully guarded against. Everybody, for example, has at some time or other been told, or discovered for himself, that he is standing too near his ball, and so cramping his hitting. To creep gradually and imperceptibly closer in, as if to woo the ball with more impassioned addresses, is the commonest fault in life, and at the same time so insidious a one that even the very greatest are sometimes its victims. How uncommon is it, on the other hand, for any one to find himself standing too far away from the ball; it is so rare a vice as to be almost a virtue, certainly by far the most amiable of all golfing weaknesses.

Again, it is far commoner to exaggerate the open than the square stance; the golfer's right foot is always prone to encroach, scarcely ever to recede. This is perhaps because the more the right foot comes stealthily forward the easier it is for the player to see, so to speak, where he is going, and this is a delightful sensation—until the crash comes. If the right foot recedes to any perceptible extent the player becomes instantly conscious of the awkward feeling of hitting to square-leg, and after an uncomfortable wriggle or two generally gets back to his normal stance before worse befalls him. This is, of course, if his ordinary ambition is to hit the ball perfectly straight with neither hook nor slice. If he is one of those who stand deliberately for a hook, he will not so soon become aware of his departure from the normal ; rather by means of a little additional wrench of his shoulders will he possibly hit some particularly glorious shots, and so postpone for a while the evil day. Finally, to give one more example, it is much more necessary for a player to be on his guard against placing the ball too far back than too far forward. The latter fault he can immediately detect, but when he is enjoying one of those rare days on which he feels that nothing matters and he can address the ball in any attitude he pleases, it is fatally easy to put the ball further and further back and nearer to the right foot without any premonition of disaster. In this preliminary matter of the stance it is possible that the author of the " Art of Golf " may have had a bad influence on some young players. He was never weary of discouraging them from taking too keen an intellectual pleasure in their game and from letting their imaginations run riot in theories at the expense of practice. With this end in view he dinned into his readers' ears one short piece of advice, applicable to every

known form of breakdown—" Aim more carefully." Taken with the rest of the author's
sermon against futile style-hunting it is admirable advice, since it will persuade the broken-
down golfer to think of the ball rather than
of the vagaries of his own limbs and to thump
laboriously at it with a single mind. On the
other hand, torn from its context it is likely
to do more harm than good by inducing that
too meticulous exactitude of stance that ends
in reducing the victim to a state of paralytic
and impotent rigidity.

Nevertheless, while it is a mistake to think
too much about the art of aiming, there is no
doubt that to aim straight is not quite so easy
a matter as it would appear. All but the
supremely gifted or the supremely phlegmatic
must have been through whole days in which
the face of the club, as if imbued with a spirit
of impish mischief, resolutely declined to look
in the right direction. This, like most other
golfing ailments, is an almost entirely mental
disease, as is shown by the fact of its becoming far more acute whenever a shot has to be
played along an especially narrow strip of turf.
Every golfer knows certain holes at which
he is particularly liable to a severe attack of
shuffling and wriggling of the feet. For example,
there is the 17th hole at Formby, a hole at first
sight flat and featureless, yet in reality both
good and difficult. A perfectly straight high-
road of turf, unbroken by bunkers, leads from
tee to hole ; on the right and left-hand sides
respectively there run also perfectly straight,
like pavements by the edge of the highway,
an out-of-bounds fence and a ditch. Another
such hole was the 15th at Woking at the time
when it deservedly earned its name of Harley

Street and before the continuity of its lines had been broken by highly ingenious landscape gardening. Such holes as these, when there is nothing in the way and all the trouble lurks at the sides, are pre-eminently distracting to the bad aimer. It is recorded of a famous judge that he once tried a farmer for shooting a boy who was robbing an apple tree and that he summed up the case in these words :—" The prisoner says he aimed at nothing. Unfortunately he missed it." Most golfers are like that unlucky prisoner ; if they aim at nothing they nearly always miss it.

Of genuine bad aiming, physical rather than mental, there are naturally two varieties, aiming too much to the left and too much to the right. To speak broadly, the first is the fault of the bad player, the second of the good. The bad player aims to the left because from bitter experience he has a well-founded apprehension of a slice, and after wrestling with it for years he has at last given in and humbly made allowance for it. In one sense he cannot be said to be aiming badly, because although his direction is hopelessly wrong it is the direction that he intends. To aim to the right of the straight line is usually a different matter ; the player, while intending to aim slightly to the right to allow for an intentional hook, comes to do so, as was said before, to an extent of which he is quite unconscious. While this is an extremely insidious fault, in that it may be so unconsciously contracted, it ought not, when once discovered, to be so very difficult to cure, because deliberate hooking generally goes with pressing, and a gentler method of hitting will often remedy one fault as well as the other.

If bad aiming is an occasional fault in the longer shots, it is a painfully frequent one on the green, the days on which one can see no sort of line being innumerable as compared with those upon which a beneficent furrow seems to lead from ball to hole. There are some who hold this curious error to proceed from the mind, and others who attribute it wholly to the feet. The truth probably lies somewhere between these two extreme theories, and for the second of the two it may at least be said that a slight variation of stance makes more difference to the player's sensations in putting than in any other stroke. It is also quite common in putting to acquire the habit of facing the club too far out to the right. Exactly why this should be so it is difficult to explain, but the hands have an unpleasant knack of creeping forward and so of pushing outward the toe of the club. It is conceivable, though this is the merest suggestion, that from this wrong beginning proceeds the commonest of all putting faults, the taking of the club back with a curl inwards towards the legs. In this regard it is noteworthy that many good putters look as if they were aiming rather to the left of the hole and then push the ball slightly outwards from them. They at any rate avoid this fault of facing the club outward. It is one that should *prima facie* be very simply remediable, since it seems absurdly easy to get the club face at right angles with the line of the put. Unfortunately, it is also absurdly easy to adjust all the preliminaries with mathematical precision and then to miss the ball.

Bound up with these questions of stance and aim is the highly mysterious and not uninteresting one of preliminary waggle. The non-golfer always and the golfer sometimes (more especially when he is kept back by a slow and florid player) declares that the waggle is a gratuitous piece of folly. If there was any lesson to be learnt from a recent blindfold match, beyond that of the essentially tiresome character of such exhibitions, it was that the waggle does serve some real purpose. Toogood waggled while taking up his stance with his eyes open ; then he had to rest his club motionless behind the ball during the quite appreciable time occupied by the blindfolding, and it was by that compulsory pause that he seemed to lose in a great measure the rhythm of the stroke. If after having waggled in the ordinary manner he could merely have shut his eyes, instead of being blindfolded, and so have swung his club up without any real pause, he would—or so, at least, one felt convinced in looking at him— have swung his club far more smoothly, and, if one may so call it, harmoniously. As it was, there was a decided snatch or jump about his swing, by no means characteristic of his normal method.

It was not long ago that Mr. Hutchinson, in some comparisons between amateurs and professionals, wrote that the professional was as a rule more skilled than the amateur in making this preliminary waggle of direct assistance to the rhythm and timing of the stroke. He added that the momentary pause, when the club rests behind the ball after the waggle and before the stroke, should be adapted to the nature of the shot to be played, the longer shot demanding the shorter pause. Spectators became the more firmly persuaded of the truth of these remarks in watching Toogood having to struggle against his natural instincts in driving. Many golfers, although without being blindfolded, rob themselves in the same way of all the assistance that they might derive from addressing the ball. After preliminaries that vary with individual idiosyncrasies, they one and all settle down into a cataleptic state before finally swinging, and this condition lasts so long that their rigid muscles must entirely forget that they were ever allowed the agreeable freedom of a waggle. This method has only one merit, that of irritating the adversary, who feels as if he were hanging on the mark in some nightmare race and waiting for a phantom pistol.

The discovery has probably been made by most people at some time or other that they can, for the moment, at least, materially affect their swing by slightly altering their waggle, even though it be an alteration visible to no other eye but theirs. A discreet curbing of the waggle may be more effective than a deliberately slow swinging of the club, while, although this is much less likely, a little added ferocity and flourish of the wrists may restore to life a flaccid and impotent swing. Waggles may be seen on any day and on any course which are almost hopelessly inimical to any rhythm in hitting. Chief among these, although not so often to be seen as formerly, is the style of address called in the Badminton Library the " disappointment," wherein the player aims by means of a series of full swings, stopping the club behind the ball with a vicious jerk just as the onlooker imagines that he is going to hit it. After this it is only natural that the club-head should stop almost as it reaches the ball ; that it should go smoothly through is unthinkable.

If, however, it is possible entirely to condemn some of the preliminary flourishes of bad players, it is almost impossible to deduce from those of the very best any fixed rule. Some have cut down the waggle to the irreducible minimum appearing indeed as if they only indulged in it at all as a concession to orthodoxy. Of such are Ray and Massy and in a still more noticeable degree Duncan, and their brevity is *prima facie* a most commendable quality; but to imitate Duncan's address would certainly bring disaster to the less talented. It is so quick that with ordinary mortals a quick, jerky swing would inevitably follow; even Duncan himself, if he ever errs, almost always does so in the direction of "snatching" at the ball. At the opposite pole is Herd, who seems by his sequence of flourishes, growing more and more rapid, to be gradually lashing himself into a fury before finally hurling himself at the ball. The late Mr. F. G. Tait had something the same appearance of working himself up for a final effort, although his was an infinitely more gentle and deliberate manner of doing so.

For some occult reason even the best of amateurs spend perceptibly more time in waggling than do the professionals. Mr. Hilton, for example, is quite leisurely in his preliminaries, taking great pains to place his feet and club in exactly the right places. Mr. Maxwell's method could hardly be called leisurely; he has a decidedly florid manner of address, which grows fiercer and more menacing with each succeeding flourish, and much the same may be said of Mr. Hutchinson, who once wrote of himself as being "painfully conscious of exuberance of waggle." Mr. John Ball wastes no time in getting to work, but, save for one or two exceptions, it is only amongst the artisan golfers of Scotland that one sees that supremely confident and rapid address which is one of the hall-marks of the professional.

The precise cause of this curious difference must remain a mystery, but there is one fact connected with it which the struggling amateur of a lower grade might study with advantage before proceeding to ruin his game for ever by trying vainly to emulate Duncan. Some of the best amateurs may waggle, to speak comparatively, with prodigality, but they waggle uniformly. The process may be an elaborate one, but it scarcely ever varies, and any one who knows their game is not left in doubt as to the exact moment at which they will hit the ball. The inferior player who waggles to excess has something of the appearance of a timid bather about to dive, who at the last moment thinks that the water looks cold and uninviting, and seeks a fresh stock of bravery by poising himself anew. For him the waggle is one long-drawn-out agony of doubt ; his courage ebbs and flows with each wave of the club, and the psychological moment for hitting seems always to have just gone by. There is little trace of this in the styles of amateurs above quoted ; their minds are as firmly made up as those of the professionals, but their bodies for some reason do not respond so quickly. This is not to say that an address that is uniform and brief is not better than one that is uniform and slow. If it can be attained with any degree of comfort it must surely be better, if only for the reason that it gives less time for intelligent thought to obtrude itself, and how many strokes have been ruined by thinking no man can say.

VI.

GOLF AND THE WEATHER.

Lord Avebury has somewhere observed that there is no such thing as bad weather, but only different kinds of good weather. This profound remark will appeal to many golfers who, with questionable wisdom, play their game in all sorts and conditions of weather and all the year round. They will play in the snow with red balls, and they even played through the broiling and intolerable summer of 1911.

This last was indeed a true test of enthusiasm, for to less heroic persons there are under such circumstances but two bearable moments in the round; there is one—only a temporary surcease from sorrow—at the " ginger-beer hole," and another, of infinite relief, when the ball of one party or the other totters into the 18th hole. The rest is like a bad dream; nor is the so-called cool of the evening much to be preferred. It is not merely the physical discomfort attending a process of slow grilling that is so exceedingly unpleasant; the dusty ground, the bare, slippery tees, and brown greens—these would make a detestable game of it even on a winter's day. Almost the only people to be pleased are those possessing unique powers of self-deception as to the lengthening of their drives, and they indeed would probably believe that they had at last discovered the eternal secret of long hitting were they to practise upon a frozen lake. The

best that can be said is that a few cross-bunkers,
which would in normal conditions be dull, now
become searching tests of skill. There is a
certain fascination in the playing of a shot
wherein the ball must be heavily cut and pitched
not more than 6ft. over the bunker if disaster
is not to ensue. Yet for one cross-bunker that
is thus rendered interesting half-a-dozen are made
ridiculous, or rather are made interesting in a
manner hardly consistent with their dignity,
since the only possible course is to attempt the
bouncing of them. On one course whereat
the writer was so unwise as to play during that
tremendous summer there is a hole at which
the green is guarded by a narrow ditch. The
green slopes rather steeply up hill from the ditch,
yet even so the only ball which ever ended its
mad career in any reasonable proximity to the
hole cleared the ditch not at the first but at the
second bounce. To calculate the course of an
approach shot to the second bounce is by no means
an easy thing to do ; yet such is ingrained prejudice
that an opponent whose ball jumps a bunker will
scarcely escape obloquy, while his declaration
that he " played for it " only adds insult to injury.

Putting becomes largely a question of com-
pensation. To make up for the bareness and
bumpiness of the greens the ground becomes so
hard that the green keeper and his hole-cutting
machine are powerless ; the hole grows daily
larger, more worn at the edges, and easier to
get into. What Sir Walter Simpson called the
catching power of the hole becomes so greatly
increased that any one who had the courage to
hit his put hard could probably astonish himself
and disgust his opponent. To play consistently
for a " gobble " upon sun-burned greens, however,
requires a courage that is quite superhuman.

GOLF AND THE WEATHER.

While golf in these conditions is certainly not a very attractive game, it is very far indeed from being an unskilful one. There is a disposition to assert that with the ground like a rock a bad shot is as good as a good shot, and that all men are equal, but this is a most fallacious belief. No doubt as between two players of widely differing degrees of merit the hard ground does tell very perceptibly in favour of the weaker; he gains in length a number of strokes for which nothing can quite compensate the giver of odds. On the other hand, in the case of two players more or less equally matched the better man ought to have no great cause for lamentation. At Prestwick in the Amateur Championship of 1911 the conditions were such as are usually spoken of as being pre-eminently "fluky," but they produced the best player beyond all manner of doubt as the winner; what is more, Mr. Hilton not only won, but he won nearly all his matches with ridiculous ease.

The test of skill, if quite as severe, is decidedly different from that supplied by normal conditions; it is one that will always be considered by the more conspicuously manly to be of a rather "niggling" character. Straightness becomes more than ever important, and discreet shortness may become a virtue; the approach shot is no longer played with the noble and straightforward motive of getting the ball into the hole, but with the comparatively sneaking and ungentlemanly one of getting it on the right side of the hole. A good example was provided by the 9th hole at Prestwick. Many a player played what he was pleased to call the best second shot that ever was struck; the ball came to rest some five or six yards above the hole and three puts were the inevitable consequence. The really good second shot was in fact that which brought the ball to rest some ten or a dozen yards below the hole, and it is noteworthy that throughout his matches Mr. Hilton was never past the hole with his second, and never lost it. To be able to play a hole time after time with this deliberate moderation shows a wonderful control alike of self and of the club ; it is a performance not only skilful, but essentially brave, because, although most of the shots that are short come from lack of courage, yet to be deliberately short requires plenty of determination.

Another feature that makes approaching upon hard ground so excessively difficult is the necessity for fixing on a certain spot of ground for the ball to pitch upon. With the ground soft there is no such necessity ; all that there is to do is to pitch the ball practically up to the flag ; the flag guides the eye and does the marking of the spot for one. When one has to discover the spot for oneself, allowing for the proper amount of run, and then keep that spot in the mind's eye while keeping the actual eye upon the ball, the affair becomes far more complex and the temptation to play a weak and nerveless sort of stroke is enormously increased. Altogether it must be frankly admitted that golf during a heat-wave is as skilful a game as need be. At the same time it is not nearly such a good game, in the ordinary sense of the word, as it is when the ground is softer. Hence the golfer may well pray for rain, whether on behalf of champions or of ordinary mortals.

When at length the merciful rain does come tempers in the aggregate are better and scores lower. The improvement in their game the players will attribute rightly enough to the disappearance of the sun, but they will possibly lay undue stress upon the rain's beneficial effect upon themselves and hardly think enough of its effect on the ground. At the risk of some disillusionment it may be laid down that golf becomes very nearly as easy a game as it can ever be. Though slightly curtailed in the matter of run, the cleanly struck ball still goes such a distance as to make the expression " two-shot hole " a hollow mockery, while the ensuing mashie shot is through the partial softening of the turf incomparably easier. The player fondly imagines that he has suddenly and miraculously recovered his pitching ; let him tear the veil from his eyes and see himself as he is, or rather as he was but a day or two ago—a poor creature, fearful lest the hard ground should jar the club from out his hands ; without the skill to pitch the ball on the green and make it stop there, yet lacking courage to pitch short of the hazard and trust to fortune and the rubber-cored ball. When the ground through the green is fairly hard and the putting greens themselves are well watered, the golfer comes as near as it is possible in this world to eating his cake and having it.

Then, too, the putting becomes much easier ; that is, if the wielders of the mowing machine have been reasonably energetic and have set to work upon the greens, which, after the first deluge, are apt to be rough and tufty. The one little disappointment is that the holes appear unaccountably to have shrunk, since the ball has now to deal with a new, clean-cut hole, and no longer with the well-worn frayed and friendly edge of an old one. The rain has by no means made the greens really slow ; it has only taken off the excessive polish, and many would perhaps prefer them, for greater facility of holing, a good deal slower still. Different people like greens of very different paces, and each member of the large class of putters afflicted with the disease of moving their bodies at the wrong moment doubtless prefers just that pace which reduces the temptation of body-moving in his particular case to a minimum. This temptation is generally greatest when the greens are either very fast or very slow, though for a different reason in each case. When the greens are very keen the player is apt to bring his club to the ball in so slow and gingerly a fashion that at one moment there seems a danger of things coming altogether to a standstill ; the body, with a sort of sub-conscious desire to accelerate matters, makes a lurch forward and the club head gets left behind with disastrous results. On the other hand, when the grass is soft and velvety he is seized with an unreasoning terror lest by means of wrists alone he should not be able to hit the ball hard enough, wherefore he throws his misguided body into the stroke to make up the balance of strength. A pace that is somewhere between the two extremes may minimize this horrible temptation, though nothing can do away with it ; it is always lurking in wait for the putter who has lost ever so little of his confidence.

How different to the pleasing sensations produced by the first shower are those produced by the first big wind that blows after many still and stifling days. The first gale of autumn dissipates with its shrewd blasts many cherished illusions, and awakens people once more to the fact that slicing and pulling do not always denote a complete and wonderful mastery over the club.

GOLF AND THE WEATHER.

Pulling is a vice that has always something of manliness about it; however lamentable the result from a half-crown winning point of view, one can at any rate boast of the distance that the ball has flown in the wrong direction, but to aim towards mid-on and then to see the ball floating away far over the head of cover-point is always humiliating. In the former case there is some scope for pretending that one could have hit straight by exercising a measure of paltry caution; in the latter no such delusion is possible.

There are courses, however, where even the most self-satisfied of hookers cannot long maintain his complacency. The writer remembers with peculiar vividness one autumn gale at Rye, which is certainly one of the most notable of these courses. At each of the first three holes a ball that is pulled at all seriously from the tee inevitably goes into or over a ditch that is out of bounds, and with a strong gale blowing from right to left the influence possessed by that one little stagnant ditch is positively magnetic. Perhaps no one of these three tee shots is quite so alarming as that at the tenth, where it is the sliced and not the pulled ball that is whirled out of bounds; but it is doubtful whether this tenth hole claims so many victims as do the others. It is only the very brave and very skilful player who dares to take any liberties with a hurricane blowing on his back. The ordinarily weak mortal realizes that to treat a slicing wind as a friend rather than an enemy is to tempt Providence too far; not daring to make allowance for the slice, he tries to hook his ball right into the eye of the wind, being content to make a great sacrifice of distance if only he can avoid destruction. With a wind that blows from right to left the case is rather different. A player of quite modest attainments can often make great use of such a wind by playing with just a little hook; it is, compared with the other, an easy thing to do. He knows the delicious feeling of the right wrist turning over just after the ball is struck and the spectacle of that ball, endowed with apparently unlimited running powers, scurrying away into the far distance. He will not give up these joys and the sense of mastery over the elements that they bring; and for this not wholly ignoble weakness he very often pays the penalty of three balls in three different portions of the ditch.

There never was such a course as Rye for cross-winds. There is one hole at which the wind is dead against the player, and one where it bowls him and his ball light-heartedly along before it; at the other sixteen it deals him a series of violent buffets either on one side or the other. The one hole where the wind is, as a rule, an honest, straightforward adversary, is the eleventh. At the fourteenth, where it poses as a friend, it is really an enemy in disguise; for there is sandy ground just in front of the green and a deep bunker behind it, and to pitch the ball on the green, so as to make it stop there, requires a mixture of genius and good fortune. At every other hole it is a matter of aiming far to the left or far to the right, as the case may be, trying to stand steady on the feet for one brief moment, and then hoping for the best. For one day or even two it is a splendid discipline and adds a zest to life; more than two days of it are apt to knock the swing to pieces, so that it is no longer worthy of the name.

If those who play by the sea can have too much wind those who play near London in the winter can assuredly have too much fog. Even those who possess almost superhuman powers of concentration and have believed themselves hitherto to be wholly engrossed in beating their ball or their adversary, utterly regardless of the beauties of Nature, discover that a view, even though they never consciously look at it, does add to the sum of their pleasures. Then, too, the ground is just a little more sticky, the worm-casts a little more plentiful, and the ball lies more unpleasantly close in misty weather than in any other, while the difficulties of aiming at something one cannot see are too obvious to enumerate.

Yet wonderful things have been done in a fog. "One misty moisty morning" Braid came home at Walton Heath in the really ridiculous score of 31 ; and soon afterwards on the same course he played two successive rounds of 69 and 71, though he could not see a hundred yards in front of him. Moreover, in their own humbler way many golfers have probably surprised themselves by the accuracy and even brilliance of their play in similar circumstances. It may almost be said that driving from the tee is actually easier in a fog than on a clear day ; the ball does not fly quite so far through the moist and heavy air, but it makes ample amends by a refreshing straightness. From this fact there is a very evident moral to be drawn—namely, that there is much virtue in singleness of purpose. In a fog the golfer contents himself with facing, roughly, in what he believes to be the right direction and then launches the ball upon its voyage ; he may not altogether obliterate from his too active mind the existence of a bunker hidden somewhere in the wreaths of mist, but out of sight is, to some extent, out of mind. If he saw the bunker he would wriggle uneasily on his feet and aim just a little further to right or left to make sure of avoiding it ; and it is this futile endeavour to make perfectly certain of safety that causes innumerable disasters. As it is he aims straight in front of him, trusting more in Providence and less in himself. This singleness of mind affects more than the mere act of aiming. It induces a certain brutish stupidity, of infinite usefulness, wherein right and left toes, flat and upright swings are seen for once in their proper relation to the main object of hitting the ball. A squall of rain or wind, a snowstorm, and a fog have this one common merit—that they occupy the golfer's mind so fully that he has no time to think about his style.

Not only is it rather easy than otherwise to drive straight in a fog, but the long shots through the green, whether with brassey, cleek, or iron, are often surprisingly successful. So long as a man is hitting, roughly speaking, as hard as he can with any club, blindness and ignorance may help rather than hinder him. But once he comes to play what is vaguely called an approach shot, when he is trying to pitch his ball on a particular spot and to hit it with a particular strength, then he may revile the fog justifiably and wholeheartedly. He will not even have the consolation of being unable to see the bunkers, for their shapes will loom upon his horizon all the more terrible from their dimness. The outstanding virtue of a good approacher is that he hits the ball firmly and crisply, and nothing makes it so hopelessly difficult of attainment as uncertainty of mind. If the player can harden his heart in these circumstances he will probably find that out of sheer ignorance he is often past the hole with his iron shots, and if this should surprise him, then he can deduce from that fact another obvious moral to help him on the next fine day.

If fog were all, things would be bad enough, but too often the barometer rises unpleasantly high, non-golfers become unpleasantly brisk, hearty, and self-satisfied, and there is the additional and painful possibility of golf in a frost, for which there is absolutely nothing to be said. It is true that when Mr. de Montmorency accomplished his two wonderful rounds of 71 in a single day at Rye the greens were crisp with frost, but this is merely the exception that proves the rule that golf on frozen ground is an impossibility and an abomination. The wisest course is to put one's clubs resolutely away, and pray that the date of the skating championship may speedily be announced, since this is the only way so far ascertained with any certainty of inducing a thaw.

If golfers will insist on playing in a frost there is one pitfall that they should be warned against : they must try to keep a level head on the subject of their driving. It is so very difficult to believe quite sincerely that the prodigious distances driven are solely due to the state of the ground. That the iron-hard turf has something to do with it the golfer will admit, but he cannot altogether stifle the belief that he has discovered something, just the faintest suggestion of a new style, about his hitting that has added on a few more yards. He may have begun the day with a mind serene and unclouded by theory, but after a few stupendous drives he cannot help wondering what it is that he is doing so particularly right, and this is even more fatal than wondering what is particularly wrong. Let him then go out to play, if he must play, with this firm conviction : that nobody is likely to drive his best when he is swathed in waistcoats, when his hands are frozen, and his feet slip on the tee. If he can really believe this in his heart there is hope for him still.

VII.

MODERN DEVELOPMENTS.

There is no doubt whatever as to the true blue principles of the golfing conservative. He objects, roughly speaking, to every tendency to innovation that has showed itself since the popularity of golf first began to spread with such amazing swiftness. Sometimes he is quite right and the English golfer must with shame admit that a number of his compatriots have done their best to degrade and vulgarize the game. Sometimes, on the other hand, he appears exceedingly unreasonable, and in every case it is probably well to remember that ours is a free and glorious country in which no man need play golf with a person or in a method distasteful to him. Let us glance for a moment with a mildly conservative eye at some of those innovations which excite the most violent hostility. There is the huge number of handicaps, Bogey and everything to do with him, four-ball matches, more especially when they are ignorantly called " four-ball foursomes," and the plethora of team matches. Of these Bogey undoubtedly constitutes the head and front of the modern golfer's offending.

At the moment of writing an event is about to occur which Sir Leicester Dedlock, had he been a golfer, would have considered an example of " the obliteration of landmarks, the opening of floodgates, and the uprooting of distinctions."

The Royal and Ancient Club is to consider the giving to the world of an official code of rules for Bogey play, a form of competition which it has hitherto rigidly ignored. This is quite in accord with the painstaking and conciliatory attitude which has happily become characteristic of St. Andrews ; there is no loss but rather a gain of dignity involved, and there may thus be an end to many murmurings.

One may subscribe to these comparatively revolutionary sentiments while not weakening in the slightest in a personal dislike to Bogey, but if a large majority of golfers desire to amuse themselves in this way peace and quiet can be cheaply bought by giving them rules whereby to guide themselves. Moreover, even the most inveterate of conservatives would probably admit that, apart from its name, a Bogey competition is an infinitely harmless amusement, putting a less painful strain on the nerves than does a medal competition, while affording an equally good chance of acquiring one of those prizes generically and contemptuously classed as butter-dishes.

The chief and most eminently reasonable objection to Bogey is the practical impossibility of devising a satisfactory score for him, a task which grows more hopeless every year. With a gutty ball, and even with the earlier rubber-cored ball, it was possible to say of a certain number of holes that they could not be reached in two strokes ; at any rate they could not be reached by a player of such contemptible, although too often unattainable, mediocrity as Bogey. Now, however, that even the more senile can drive a ball something over 200 yards there is hardly such a thing as a hole that ought to be done in 5 ; they all ought to be done in 4, although they are very often done in 7. Consequently Bogey, who does not deal in fractions, must be allotted 5 for some holes and 4 for others, although almost the only discernible principle of allotment is that if he did nothing but 4's he would play far too well, and if nothing but 5's far too badly. The very excellent course at Stoke Poges comes to mind as a good instance. The man who should hit all his shots a good but not enormous distance with perfect straightness and hole out in two puts on each green ought to have a round consisting of fourteen 4's and four 3's, but such a score represents in fact absolutely wonderful play. Yet, save in the case of the 4th and 17th holes, there is no particular reason for turning any one of the 4's into a 5. Nor again is there any reason for allowing 4 at one of the short holes rather than at any of the other three. All the holes are good and difficult, and a good player will fall away from perfection at some of them, not because they are more difficult than others, but simply because he is a fallible human being. It is one of the obvious defects of Bogey that he is far too gross in his methods ; he cannot allow for any shades of difference that are in the least degree subtle.

This is undeniably the weak point of Colonel Bogey as a medium for competitions, but it is no sufficient cause for violent anger. That which does justifiably make many otherwise placid citizens rage with scorn and fury, is the base use to which his score is put by some of his devotees. They regulate their entire ideas of any particular hole, its merits or demerits and the way in which it should be played, not by such intelligence as they chance to possess, but merely by the number of strokes assigned to the hole in an imaginary score, that score being frankly and obviously the merest compromise made between the unattainably good and the moderately bad. A "Bogey 5" may mean a hole of such a length that it can be reached with a drive and an iron shot, or it may demand two drives and a pitch. Yet there are hundreds of golfers gifted with intellects so curious that they deem the doing of a 4 at the one an achievement exactly as meritorious as it would be at the other. When one of these singularly constituted individuals, having played a hole by means of five most indifferent strokes, pats himself metaphorically on the back because the hole is a Bogey 5, the irritation produced is but slight; it is possible to say to oneself that if this rather fatuous person is pleased there is no real reason for any one else to be otherwise. Patience, however, has its limits, and if the golfer who has played the indifferent five strokes is oneself, and this idiotic form of consolation is administered by an opponent, then anger is apt to boil over.

A discussion once took place as to the proposed putting forward of a certain tee by a comparatively small number of yards. It was generally agreed that the hole would be improved out of all knowledge, since two good and difficult strokes would be required to reach the green instead of three dull and featureless ones; but this objection was gravely raised by one party, "Would not it make it rather a short hole for a Bogey 6?" Comment is superfluous, but it is observations of this sort rather than the nature of the competition itself that have fostered in many breasts such an implacable hatred to Bogey and Bogey-worship.

To handicapping in general not even the most crusted may be presumed to object, but it is legitimate to object to the much exaggerated importance often attached to it. Handicaps are primarily made for special competitions, and in addition they are useful, between two strangers, as rough indications of form. Beyond this point their usefulness need not be pushed, and the idea of having one vast list of handicaps for all the golfers in the kingdom is entirely to be deprecated. Not long ago the Yorkshire Union attempted the task of co-ordinating or standardizing the handicaps of the union clubs. In order to attain this object each club was required to send in a return showing the length of the holes on its course and allowing a certain score for each, 3, $3\frac{1}{2}$, 4, $4\frac{1}{2}$, 5, $5\frac{1}{2}$, or 6, " according to length." It was proposed thus to obtain the " par " score of each course ; then to add to this score 3, 4, or 5 strokes in order to get the " scratch " score, which should form the basis of the handicap. The matter has not yet apparently passed the experimental stage and the experiment has not, as one would imagine, been received with any wild outburst of enthusiasm, since 33 out of the 69 clubs failed to send in the required return.

It seems very doubtful whether this standardizing of handicaps can ever be done satisfactorily, even if it is in the very least degree worth doing at all. It has often been pointed out that no form of statistics is more fallacious than are " par " scores. A hole which bristles with bunkers and demands two full shots, both of the nicest accuracy, is a " par 4 " ; so is the most featureless and contemptible hole of the drive and pitch variety, 250 yards long and with never a bunker in sight. Yet these two holes are in regard to the skill demanded of the player as the poles asunder. This is, of course, a commonplace of criticism, and the Yorkshire Union has attempted to get over the difficulty by reckoning in half strokes. But such a plan cannot be called satisfactory, more especially as the scores for the various holes are to be allotted " according to length," and length is only one of the various qualities of a golfing hole, none of which can be appraised in this cut-and-dried fashion. The system does not allow for difficult bunkers, tortuous greens, persistent winds, or any of those things which indubitably make one course harder than another, even though the difference cannot be reckoned in vulgar fractions.

Even if the system were to approach a great deal more nearly to perfection than any human system is at all likely to, the advisability of adopting it would be very questionable. Would not this ticketing of all the players in a county with official handicaps merely conduce to additional solemnity and fussiness on a subject about which people are quite fussy and solemn enough already ?

An innovation of handicapping, as far as golf is concerned, is the bisque, and an excellent one it is, all the more so because it has no place in official lists or medal competitions, and figures only in matches between friend and friend. Its merits are not yet as widely known as they ought to be and at present perhaps it is too often regarded as belonging of necessity to the after-luncheon period of the day, when amusing rather than strenuous golf is desired. It is rather difficult to say why this should be so, because the game ought really to be no more productive of hilarity than any other form of golf; if it be amusing at all it is only so in the way that the game of cat and mouse is amusing—very good fun for the cat. For the mouse it is the hardest of hard work, and it is one of the merits of the bisque game that the usually arrogant giver of points on this occasion plays the part of the mouse, and for the first few holes, at any rate, feels that he is being toyed with in a most unpleasant manner. The giver of points has so much the better of it in match play—for one thing he nearly always wins—that any plan that shall give him even a bad quarter of an hour is to be welcomed, and so much at least the recipient of bisques should always be able to achieve. If he cannot do it by the more artistic slow torture of holding bisques in reserve as long as possible, he can at least accomplish something by a prodigal and overwhelming display at the start; he can put his man two or three holes down to begin with, and when once one has got a man three down there is always hope; one may thereafter play very badly oneself, but the enemy may by that time have been battered and cowed into playing worse.

This plan of trying to crush the manly spirit of the enemy at the first outset is not, however, one to be generally recommended; to do so is generally to play into the opponent's hands. It will nearly always be seen that the giver of bisques is anxious for them to be taken at the earliest possible moment; and after a half at the very first hole he will ask, with but an ill-simulated carelessness, "Do you take a bisque there?" So long as the bisques are held up he never quite knows what his position is; he feels that he is only leading in the race on sufferance, and is for ever glancing uneasily back over his shoulder at his pursuer. It will be observed, moreover, that those who from a tennis education are familiar with the use of bisques are always chary of encroaching on their store until they are absolutely driven to it.

The most obvious advantage of bisques is, of course, that he who receives them is certain of reaping the full advantage of his handicap. When he receives strokes at fixed holes he may in a sense waste a large proportion of them, but only the most ill-judged penuriousness can deprive him of the use of a single bisque. Moreover, although in this the game only panders to his vanity, he can have the satisfaction of winning the game without using any or some of his allowance. When strokes are given in the ordinary way a golfer will often be heard to boast that he won without using his strokes, but nobody pays the slightest attention to his vapourings; it is recognized that, whatever the actual figures, the strokes may have largely affected the play at their particular holes. A bisque, on the other hand having a moral influence much more widely diffused, and so less capable of being accurately estimated, may by common consent be legitimately stored up and made a boast of. Altogether this game of bisques is one which is strongly to be recommended to the weaker vessel, so long as he can obtain two bisques for every three strokes of his ordinary allowance. Bisques are valuable, but not so valuable as scratch players are apt to make them out, and to accept less would be to " fall into the vulgar error of not taking enough."

Now we come in our list of modern developments to two that are good enough in moderation but thoroughly bad in excess, four-ball matches and team matches. The question of the respective merits from the player's point of view of a foursome and a four-ball match is too ancient and too polemical a one for discussion, but the shortcomings of the latter as an entertainment for spectators may perhaps be pointed out. In nearly all exhibitions the programme takes the same form. In the morning Vardon and Braid, or some other two champions, play a round by score play, and in the afternoon they are joined by two local celebrities in a four-ball match. That a contest by score should take the place of a match proper is no doubt due to the frenzied desire for a " record " by a champion, and it is likely enough that the duel between the two professionals will be equally close and interesting by whichever method it is decided ; but as regards the four-ball match it may be suggested that club committees do not understand their business as showmen.

Perhaps the best " show," as opposed to a match in a tournament, that the writer remembers to have seen in the last few years was a 36-hole foursome played at Sheringham between Braid and Vardon on the one side, and Taylor and Massy on the other. The play was followed with the greatest interest by a large crowd, all of whom, except those who had scarcely seen golf played before, appeared to know at any particular point how the match stood. On the evening before this match the four players played a practice round in a four-ball match, and the contrast between these two days' play was remarkable. In the four-ball match, played at a tremendous pace, there was hardly ever time properly to watch one man play his stroke, because the eye was distracted by the sight of three more just about to play theirs. Which side was winning or losing it was exceedingly difficult to tell, and the remarks heard among the onlookers showed that not one in ten of them had the very dimmest idea on this not unimportant point.

In watching good golfers it is interesting to see first the way in which they make their strokes and secondly which of them wins the holes. A four-ball match renders it nearly impossible to do either. In the case of those who have never seen the best professionals play before, the only impression left on the mind is one of the general and bewildering splendour of the play; with those who are more sophisticated it is one of almost unmixed weariness. If there is on a committee one man who can make himself so unpleasant as to get his own way and insist on the professionals playing a foursome, he always earns in the end the gratitude, not only of the players, but of all his fellows. Some of these, indeed, are usually kind enough to say that they had no idea a foursome was such a good game. There are but few, however, who can make themselves unpleasant enough, and so the four-ball matches go drearily on.

The team match again which is largely bound up with the golfing society is a pleasant enough thing in its way, but it has almost been done to death. Quite lately the writer was engaged to play in two of these contests for one society against another and in each case the other side scratched from sheer inability to raise a team of eight men—an indication of, to say the least of it, very moderate enthusiasm.

The foundation of the Oxford and Cambridge Golfing Society some 13 or more years ago set a fashion which has since been very extensively followed. Singularly enough, schoolmasters, who are notoriously the most gregarious of men, have no such institution; but nearly every other profession or trade that it is possible to think of has now its own golfing society. There is, however, a difference worth pointing out between the original society and most of its imitators. The former consists not merely of people who are supposed to have been educated at Oxford or Cambridge, but for the most part of those who have played golf for one of those two Universities. Some are naturally better players than others, but most of the members come up to a certain standard as golfers. On the other hand, among the members of what may conveniently be called the professional societies there is a much greater difference in playing ability. There are highly distinguished golfers who are highly undistinguished in their profession, and there are others whose achievements in the domains of play and work are in an exactly opposite ratio. It may be suggested that this fact is rather lost sight of, and that more general entertainment could be extracted from golfing societies if it were oftener remembered.

There are, of course, exceptions, but most professional societies appear to expend the greater part of their energies upon playing matches against each other. These matches are, no doubt, moderately—and only moderately—good fun in themselves for those that play in them. If nobody minds very much who wins them, that is a disadvantage which attaches to the greater number of team matches and need not be insisted upon. But they only provide amusement for some eight or ten out of the whole strength of the society ; the captain, in duty bound and jealous for what he pleases to call the honour of his profession, chooses the best eight, and therefore the same eight, time after time, and the rank and file of the society might as well not exist. It may be added that these chosen eight are by the irony of circumstances more often than not those who least desire to play. Being good players they get as many team matches as they want for their own clubs ; and, although they obey their captain's call, it is with a mixture of resignation and loyalty rather than with any conspicuous joy.

Such a state of things seems to argue a misapprehension of the proper purposes and functions of this kind of golfing society. Its real object ought surely to be to give the members, old and young, good and bad golfers, a chance of getting to know each other better through the medium of a game just sufficiently strenuous to be agreeable. In fact a meeting of a golfing society should bring the members together in something like the mood which, in lower strata of society, finds vent in a *char-à-banc*, a gentleman with a cornet, and an ultimate beanfeast.

The annual Bar Tournament affords a good instance of the amount of entertainment that can be extracted from a society. The youngest of juniors has the opportunity of talking to the most learned of leaders and of tremulously acquiring the practice of calling him by his surname without the " Mr.," which the rule of his profession enjoins. Three or four friendly and delightful summer days are spent on a good seaside course, and while everybody wants to win, nobody suffers very acutely if he does not. To advise others to imitate this tournament would, however, be to give a counsel of perfection, since barristers get longer holidays than other people and take them at one and the same time. For less favoured mortals a meeting must be a genuine beanfeast consisting of but one day's outing, and instead of match play recourse must be had to the far less attractive medal. Nevertheless, if the medal round is played in the morning all the miseries of the day are over early, and there remain luncheon and a foursome and perhaps even a third round. Such a day at least caters for everybody, whereas the team matches only fail in endeavouring to amuse those who least need amusing.

Furthermore, the team matches might be made to give a great deal more pleasure than they do at present if it was not so regularly deemed necessary for each side to put or try to put its best side in the field. It really ought not to matter in the least how bad the sides are, if they enjoy a reasonable equality of badness such as shall conduce to a close game. If the two captains can put their heads together and agree roughly on the handicaps of the players— arranging, for instance, that each side shall have one scratch man, one with a handicap of 6, another of 12, and so on down to a blushing *débutant* with 24—they can generally make sure of obtaining eight men on each side who really want to play and do not play only because they think they ought to. Such a match provides the participants with infinitely good fun ; but then it ought not solemnly to be recorded in print as a set contest between two professional societies. The fierce light of the sporting intelligence in the morning paper terrifies each captain, so that he casts all hopes of pleasure aside and essays once more the joyless task of collecting a representative side of martyrs.

VIII.

GOLFING PSYCHOLOGY.

The man who watches many golf matches
becomes *blasé* in course of time. He is no longer
satisfied to see where the ball goes to ; he comes
to know so well every trick and method of those
who hit it that he has but to close his eyes and
at any moment he can conjure up a whole
procession of champions in characteristic atti-
tudes. Then his jaded appetite longs for some
more subtle pleasure, and that which chiefly
interests him is to watch for some indication
of those poignant and rapidly alternating emo-
tions without which scarcely any one can play a
hard match at golf. There is a certain ghoulish
satisfaction in noting the half-hearted shot
that tells its tale, in declaring that the unfortunate
player is overcome with nervousness and is
going to " crack," and in finding oneself right.
Especially is it interesting to those who, themselves cursed with highly strung temperaments,
have suffered all too often the same miseries.

The casual spectator at a golf match is often
apt to credit those whom he honours by his
notice with a degree of calmness which they are
far from possessing. At least, after seeing a
player making a series of bad shots and clearly
suffering from an agony of nervousness, one is
sometimes startled by a neighbour in the crowd
wondering whether so-and-so " is really trying."
He must know, unless he possess extraordinary

powers of self-deception, that he has himself missed many shots from purely mental causes ; but he is often slow in discovering that others, who are more skilful players, are yet equally human.

There is probably no game which affords a greater scope than golf for all possible forms of nervousness, not only for sheer terror but for every conceivable foolish fancy which can impair the properly concentrated frame of mind. It is so horribly deliberate and long drawn out that it is impossible to make the mind a blank ; and it may be safely laid down that there is not a golfer in the world who has not at times felt a paralysing sensation creeping over him. The best match-player is not the man who has never felt it—for he, if he exists, can hardly possess the keenness necessary to doing his best—but the man who can most successfully overcome it. Those who knew Mr. Travis well declared that he was by nature a nervous man ; but certainly no one ever could have divined it from the almost superhuman coolness with which he played in his memorable championship at Sandwich. There are, indeed, those who profess to be able to discover from some mysterious symptoms—the angle of his cap or the lilt of his walk—that Mr. John Ball is feeling anxious ; but to the casual observer the Amateur Champion is always the same, a man of granite, immovable.

The ordinary player, with ordinarily bad nerves, can master them far more successfully on one day than on another, and that without knowing the reason why. A comparatively short run of victories even over quite insignificant opponents is apt to breed an astonishing and most serviceable confidence. The victor may not have played more than passably well; he may not be under any particular delusion as to the merit of his performance, but still he attains that happy frame of mind in which he believes that things will come right and not wrong in the end, and that he will "muddle through" somehow. It has been said before that the man is "on his game" who does not mind making a bad shot, and this enviable state is generally produced by a run of good luck. If, on the other hand, his run has been one of bad luck, he goes to meet trouble something more than half way, and hails the first bad shot as the beginning of the end—the end both of his match and also of the particular new system of driving, pitching, or putting which with faint and trembling hope he has just invented.

One of the most distressing features of the complaint is that the victim never knows when and where it will seize him in its grip. He may begin his match by feeling, to his intense surprise, mildly bored with the proceedings; that is generally bad, since this lethargy may never wear off and he may be beaten through a sheer inability to try. Again, he may start with a magnificent and stoical calm, and all may go well for a while. Then, just when he is rejoicing in this Heaven-sent mood, he may make one mistake, and with scarcely any warning find himself prostrated by a sudden wave of nervousness. This is perhaps the worst of all things that can befall him, since it is doubly difficult to recover from the unexpected. To find himself trembling like a leaf upon the first tee, although in itself unpleasant, does not always presage disaster; for thus he sometimes suffers the worst agonies before the real struggle begins; and if things go passably well for a hole or two, he gets into his stride and maintains it to the end.

GOLFING PSYCHOLOGY.

The curious tricks that nerves can play upon their owners are particularly well illustrated by matches that go to the 19th hole. Take by way of example two of the matches in the English Ladies' Championship, played not long since at Prince's, Sandwich. Two ladies were dormy 6 and dormy 5 up respectively upon their opponents; in each case the leader lost all the remaining holes and the match was halved; then, on proceeding to the 19th (or, as in one case, to the 21st) hole, the player who had lost her long lead in so demoralizing a fashion pulled herself together and won after all. Nor is this apparently singular occurrence to be seen solely in ladies' championships, for it was only in the summer of 1911 in the American Championship that Mr. Hilton, after having stood some 5 or 6 holes up on Mr. Herreshoff, lost every single hole of his lead and won at the 37th hole. Yet another example may be given from Mr. Hilton's career. When he beat Mr. Low in the final match of the Amateur Championship at St. Andrews in 1901 he stood 5 up with 13 to play, was pulled back to all square and 2 to play, and then, by playing two holes as well as they could humanly be played, won by a single hole. In fact the occurrence is so comparatively common that, however unaccountable, it must be reckoned among the things that may be expected to happen.

Unaccountable at first sight it most certainly is. The player who lets a long lead slip away from him is always in a more or less nervous, miserable, and peevish condition; he who has snatched a match apparently lost out of the fire is, on the other hand, confident and triumphant. It would seem that the nerveracking experience of a 19th hole should only accentuate the difference between these two opposite frames of mind. Yet as a fact the tide seems as often as not to turn with these extra holes. So long as he has any lead still to dissipate the leader plays in a faint-hearted manner, as if lamenting over the irrevocable past instead of devoting himself to the present. When every hole is squandered and his back is against the wall, a sort of fierce composure seems to settle down upon him; he really concentrates his mind and really fights. But the success of this last desperate rally should not perhaps be wholly attributed to him that makes it, because the adversary has also undergone a revulsion of feeling. When he was 5 or 6 holes down he thought of avoiding, not defeat, but disgrace ; the possibility of victory itself probably did not definitely obtrude itself until very nearly the end of the round. When, however, he has wiped out the whole of that crushing deficit and faces the tee once more an unburdened man, the almost miraculous nature of his escape thrusts itself upon him ; he reflects that to lose now, after all he has gone through, would be insupportably bitter ; he falters for an instant, and in that one instant is undone. The picturesque *rôle* of the heroic and indomitable pursuer is in some ways more easy to support, so long as there seems no real chance of the pursuit being crowned with success.

Match play makes an enthralling study in that it is possible directly to contrast the temperaments of the two opponents and to see how they act and re-act upon each other, but for the study of the nervous breakdown in all its forms a scoring competition probably affords the richer field. How singularly distressing an experience

is the first medal round played after a considerable interval ? More than any other form
of golf, a scoring competition brings home the
necessity for practice ; nor is it enough that the
body should be accustomed to its task, for it is
almost equally important that the mind should be
in practice also. To play a hard match on level
terms against a formidable adversary after a
series of gentle games under handicap or jovial
after-lunch foursomes will reveal to the golfer,
with something of the same unpleasant vividness,
the inherent treachery of an untried nerve ;
but a medal competition, even though he has
no specially anxious desire to win it, will open
his eyes still more brutally and thoroughly.
In one of his pockets the unaccustomed card
seems to crackle noisily ; in the other the pencil,
swollen in his brain-sick fancy to gigantic
proportions, jolts painfully against his ribs.
It is a most disagreeable sensation, which will
pass off in time and can be partially avoided by
competing regularly and conscientiously for
monthly medals. Whether the remedy is not
worse than the disease is a question that everybody must decide for himself.

Many people will always be found to inveigh
against score play, and this is a perfectly
legitimate thing to do, so long as it is done
honestly and with absolute certainty of motive.
Nobody can complain if a golfer merely declares
that he plays golf for pleasure and does not
extract any from playing for a medal ; he has
told the truth, if not exactly the whole truth,
and the obvious inference that he does not
usually play well in a medal is there to be drawn
by any one that likes to draw it. On the other
hand, to abuse medal play solely upon the
ground that it is " not golf " is nine times out

of ten a dishonest proceeding, because in his inmost soul the abuser knows well that he would willingly swallow the affront to that rather mysterious thing called the real game of golf if only it did not make him feel so exquisitely uncomfortable. Whether match play or medal play requires the loftier kind of courage is perhaps a question for the metaphysician, but no great degree of penetration is required to see that the medal-playing kind is at any rate the rarer. There are doubtless to be found a few golfers who on the average do play actually better golf with a card and pencil than in a match; the names of two or three very fine players come readily enough to mind, but they are the rarest possible creatures compared with the hundreds and thousands of whom the converse proposition is true. Among the general run of ordinary amateurs the man who acquires a reputation as a score player does so not because he plays better, but because he can be relied on not to play ludicrously worse than usual when he has a pencil in his pocket. If only golfers in general would admit that very uncommon qualities are needed in score play, they would not perhaps be so exceedingly mendacious as to the causes of their failures.

Because there is no one single enemy to hate there is not in score play any great demand for that most heroic and attractive of all golfing qualities which makes a man clench his teeth and follow a brilliant shot of the enemy's by a still more brilliant one of his own. On the other hand, if the score player's face never sets quite so grimly at any one moment, it can never relax into a smile throughout the whole weary 18 holes. There is no peace for him; he cannot take a "breather" and play a hole with studied laziness in 7 because his opponent is obviously going to take 9. Every one shot is as important as every other. Moreover, to any one of imaginative temperament certain things which are all in the day's work in a match become in a medal really terrifying, unless he keep a very tight hold over himself. A very difficult hole towards the end of the round is not especially alarming in a match; there is always the chance that it will be the other man who will be destroyed by it. But in a medal the chance of another's misfortune is no comfort, and a hole that has great potentialities for disaster may haunt a nervous man like a nightmare throughout all the preceding ones. A bunker which, although big, is really essentially innocuous (such as the "Maiden" or the "Himalayas") assumes an altogether different appearance to the eye of the man with a card, just because of the quite remote, but also quite fatal, possibility of a topped tee shot.

Nevertheless, although the golfer may, on the eve of the medal, dream of some gigantic, black-boarded hill-top and awake raving, he will probably get over it safely enough when it comes to the point. It is on the green that the strain really tells; it is the putting that slays its ten thousands; and putting, moreover, nearly always of one kind—dismally, contemptibly short. The very last sentence in the "Art of Golf" is one of its truest and most depressing ones :—"To put well on a medal day one must be careless—advice easily given but difficult to follow until our card is hopelessly beyond the reach of human aid." The advice to put carelessly implies that the ball should be given a free and dashing blow, yet nearly every one grovels a thought nearer to the ground on a medal day and gives his ball a stiffer and more pusillanimous poke than usual. Nervousness and freedom of hitting are things, as nearly as may be, wholly incompatible.

There is one person connected with a golfing competition who, without taking any active part in it himself, may yet both suffer and inflict agonies of nervousness. This is the umpire or referee—his title is rather uncertain—who always appears to the spectators to enjoy a very easy time of it. He need not manifest the unceasing activity of his football brother; he need not even count the number of balls in an over, and there are reasonably long intervals between the strokes, during which he may, if he will, free his mind altogether from the trammels of golf. Nevertheless he is not a person altogether to be envied. He is not unlike a goalkeeper or a full-back, who may stand and shiver in the last line of defence for half an hour with nothing whatever to do, yet with the knowledge that when he is called upon to act his task may be a thoroughly unpleasant, difficult, and responsible one. He will most likely never be asked to give a decision on a simple point, for simple questions decide themselves, and players who are important enough to need an umpire have a working knowledge of the ordinary rules, and seldom contravene them. The only point he will have to decide may be of a recondite and unusual character, and few golfers have the rules sufficiently at their fingers' ends to face all possible problems with perfect confidence. There is no other game in which the ball can perform such an immense variety of strange antics; in which it may take refuge among the teeth of a grass-cutting machine. in a paper bag, a derelict hat, or even a spectator's pocket. Owing to the number of possibilities the statute law of the game is complicated, and to most people infinitely difficult to remember, but there is also such a thing as a possibility on a possibility, if one may use the strange jargon of real property law, and the perfect umpire would remember all the decisions given by the Rules of Golf Committee upon these rarer happenings. The perfect umpire, if that standard be adopted, does not exist, but those who are conscious of their imperfections can at least do something by carrying a copy of the rules of golf and of the local rules in their pockets.

A man may be a very good lawyer and a very bad judge, and the same thing is true of the umpire. The difficult decision comes to him very seldom, and yet without making any mistake in law he can rouse players and spectators alike to the extreme stages of exasperation. He may rush frantically forward and dispossess the caddie of the flag when somebody is just about to put; he may bawl at some innocent spectator whose offence is so venial that the hardened player is quite unconscious of his presence; he may insist on talking to the combatants, who wish to devote themselves entirely to the matter in hand and yet do not like to be uncivil. He may do a number of other tiresome things, which generally proceed from too much zeal and too little experience; for the man who has himself played in big matches will nearly always be found to make the best, the most silent, and the least obtrusive umpire.

Anyone who undertakes the duties of an umpire would do well to reflect that he is there primarily, of course, to see the game played according to law, but also very largely to save the players, who are often strung up to a pitch of nervousness, as much trouble and worry as possible. It is not his place to instruct the spectators as to the right and wrong way to behave on the golf course, except in so far as the wrong way is a real hindrance to the match. Almost certainly the player would rather play his stroke subject to some little inconvenience than to be compelled to wait during the delivery of a harangue to a small boy or a very old lady. In short, the umpire is not to be, in the words of Mrs. Poyser, "Welly like a cock as thinks the sun's rose o' purpose to hear him crow."

There are umpires, of a rather different but equally undesirable type, who appear to start out on their round with the conviction that both players intend, if they are given a chance, to cheat. These officials, invariably inexperienced in this particular walk of life, follow their victims like shadows, watch them with eyes that are quite patently suspicious and even sometimes go so far as to invent wholly unauthorized laws for their discomfort. One tyrannical old gentleman, who was the umpire in a match between two young professionals, entirely refused to allow the players to concede any puts to each other, and insisted on every put being holed out, even although one party had played but four strokes and the other fourteen. The players were very young, and, the old gentleman being very fierce, they submitted meekly, but the umpire certainly did not make the games any easier for them.

GOLFING PSYCHOLOGY.

It is perhaps a dangerous doctrine to enunciate that on some rare occasions the umpire should have the gift of putting the blind eye to the telescope. Rules are rules, but when the player brushes aside with his club the muddy stump of a cigarette under the mistaken impression that it is another substance, it is surely no part of the umpire's duty to make too microscopic an investigation. Whenever an investigation has to be made or a decision given it must be done quickly and confidently, for an umpire who cannot make up his mind is intensely trying to the players. It is often extremely difficult to decide which of two balls is the further from the hole ; on the putting green the tape measure is available, but at long range the umpire must just do his best, and that quickly. Some years ago two professionals were playing off a tie in a big tournament, and the match had reached the 20th hole. Both balls lays about equi-distant from the green at the range of a very long brassey shot, and a bewildered and conscientious official solemnly proposed to walk down a hill, over a gully, and up another hill in order to see whether he could give a decisive judgment by viewing the situation from the flag. Mercifully he yielded to the agonized cry of one of the players, asking him to do something, no matter what ; not, however, before he had succeeded in inflicting a maximum of nervous torture and irritation.

IX.

THE HUMOUR OF THE GAME.

The golfer is sometimes driven to wonder drearily on the subject of golfing jokes. He wonders as to the intentions of their perpetrators : whether they meant to amuse him or only those who do not play golf. He also wonders whether they have in fact succeeded in amusing anybody at all.

The golfing joker has during the last 20 years had something more than his fair chance. There was a time when the game was so strange, and therefore so ridiculous, that a picture of a stout elderly gentleman armed with a weapon bearing a faint resemblance to a hockey stick was deemed sufficiently entertaining. If in addition the stout gentleman was struck by a ball misdirected by another gentleman and the whole scene was shown in " companion " pictures, the first being whimsically called   " Fore " and the second " Aft," then, indeed, any one possessed of a shred of humour must needs have split his sides. Bogey, too, that odious creature with which the Saxon has endowed and vulgarized the game, comprised in himself a whole treasury of wit. There are still left a few persons to whom the mere existence of the game is exquisitely amusing, who take up one's wooden putter with a bright, engaging smile and inquire if it is the niblick; but these are rare and incurable cases.

Generally speaking, the days so rich in opportunity have now passed away, save, indeed, in those circles wherein moves the professional joker. He, as it would appear, lives secluded from the world in some happy spot where clubs are still called sticks, and, to judge from the frequent and ludicrous occurrence of a broken one, the rubber-cored ball has not yet ousted the gutty. There the little play upon words involved in the expression "addressing the ball" is still considered both quaint and pretty, more especially if the point is made clear to those of meaner intelligence by a picture of a player engaged in swearing.

The joker is doubtless to be pitied, but at the same time he ought soon to begin to realize that golf is no longer quite a new game. There is an ancient farce, still occasionally played, of which the entire point consists in the novelty of the telegram, and it is asking a great deal of an audience that they should be thus amused throughout a considerable part of the evening. To take a more modern instance, even the delightful Mr. Henry Straker is occasionally tedious as he crawls ostentatiously under that once strange thing, a motor-car, and the remark applies with far greater force to old golfing jokes that had not the original advantage of being made by Mr. Shaw. Those who do make them might further realize that the humour of many incidents highly entertaining to eye-witnesses cannot be transferred either by pen or pencil. It is almost always mildly amusing, except to the inordinately humane, to see an old gentleman sit abruptly down on a slide made by mischievous boys, and it may even be amusing to hear of, if we know the particular old gentleman ; but the narrative of a gentleman in the vague meeting with this misfortune can hardly be expected to raise a smile. So also it is entertaining to see our own particular friend fling his club into the topmast branches of a tree or pursue his caddie in an apoplectic manner with a niblick. It derives an added piquancy from the fact that our merriment must often be decently concealed, but it is a joke that is killed by pen and ink.

There is undoubtedly plenty of humour to be extracted from the game ; it has given rise to some delightfully amusing writing, and even the keenest golfer realizes that he, or at any rate his opponent, can make himself highly ridiculous. Yet the fact remains that the game does not lend itself to imperishable jokes that make a really wide human appeal. There are not even many well-known golfing jokes. If a census were taken, the best known would very likely be discovered to be that in which the minister declares that he must " gie it up," and on being asked " What, gie up the gowf ? " replies " Na, na, the meenistry." It was never a tremendous joke and now after the lapse of years leaves us singularly cold.

There is an abundance of quite entertaining stories, but they suffer sadly, one and all, by reproduction. Some consist of the sayings of a famous Scottish professional, and are irreproducible for several reasons. Others —by far the larger number—depend mainly on a knowledge of the scene and the *dramatis personæ*. The personal element is nearly always predominant, and this seems to be a common defect in the stories of other games. We read in the pages of the great John Nyren of Lord Frederick Beauclerk throwing his white hat on the ground in a fury and calling Tom Walker a "confounded old beast" when that "anointed clod-stumper" resolutely blocked all the good-length balls of his lordship. It is even now a very pleasant picture, but, had we known the noble and irascible bowler and the stolid countryman who defied him, we should probably be amused to a degree that we now deem impossible. Similarly it is agreeable to hear that on a certain occasion Mr. W. threw his club into a whin bush and had perforce to say to those behind him, "Will you please pass, Sir; I've lost my club." But it is only those who know Mr. W. who really enjoy this mild little story; the others, after a decent interval, are apt to think continued chucklings unjustifiable. Moreover, when the best is said for them, these jokes are analogous to that of the old gentleman and the slide; they need reinforcement by some prodigious genius either of narrator or artist. There was one man who could give perennial joy by a picture of a village cricketer with a black eye and under it that simple but immortal passage which begins, "I'ad a hover of Jackson"; but there has only been one John Leech.

Those who have to amuse people to-day would do well, both for their own sake and their victims', to pass a self-denying ordinance with regard to golf. They should deny themselves all pleasantries dealing with the missing of the ball, the breaking of clubs, or the hitting of other players, the use of profane language and Bank Holiday picnics upon putting greens; they should also endeavour to grasp the fact that a bad joke is not turned into a good one by arraying the parties in knickerbockers. Golfers, at any rate, would be profoundly thankful to them, and it is hard to believe but that the general public would bear the blow with fortitude.

X.

SOME GREAT MATCHES.

Miss CECIL LEITCH (receiving a half) v. Mr.
H. H. HILTON.
(Played at Walton Heath and Sunningdale
October 11 and 13, 1910.)

THE FIRST DAY'S PLAY.

At Walton Heath Mr. Hilton finished 1 up
after a day's play which fluctuated in a remarkable way. At one time—to be precise, at the 13th
hole in the first round—it seemed likely that
Mr. Hilton was going to gain a long lead and
that Miss Leitch was in danger of breaking down.
She nearly "cracked" but not quite, and
taking two or three chances that came to her
in the last four holes had once again made a
good match of it by luncheon time. After
luncheon Mr. Hilton again looked like drawing
away, but after playing five holes he really went
all to pieces for a while, and Miss Leitch won
hole after hole and stood 2 up at the 11th. If
any breakdown then seemed imminent it certainly
was not the lady's. However, she made a very
bad mistake; the pendulum swung round once
more, Mr. Hilton pulled himself together, and
just got ahead with the very last stroke of the
day.

It must at once be said that Miss Leitch came
out of the day's play with infinite credit. It

was not so much what she did as what she did not
do. She can, no doubt, play much better golf, but
in the circumstances she might have played so
very much worse. The ordeal was as trying a
one as could easily be conceived. The crowd
was probably as large a one as has ever been seen
on a course in the South of England ; there must
have been fully 3,000 spectators, and although
they doubtless meant very well, some of them
had a positive genius for getting in the way.
The interest and excitement were at fever heat,
and if Miss Leitch had broken down under the
strain no one could have been surprised. But
she stuck to her guns in a way that was really
splendid ; was never flurried, took plenty of
time over her strokes, and accepted the buffets
of fortune with perfect equanimity. Her driving,
taking it all round, was very fine and decidedly
long ; what is more, her length comes mostly
from her power of hitting a carrying ball, and
she does not depend much upon run. It is hard
to judge in a crowd, but it would probably be
true to say that when both players struck the
ball properly Mr. Hilton was some 20 to 25 yards
ahead. Miss Leitch's style of hitting does not,
it must be confessed, inspire too much confidence.
She stands with rather a wide stance, the knees
very stiff and the ball exceptionally far back
near the right foot. In such an attitude the
act of swinging throws a tremendous strain on
the right knee, which rather gives under her,
producing a pronounced " duck." Still, she
comes through beautifully, times the stroke well,
and has a very great power of picking up the
ball with a wooden club. Her iron club play
was good without being very good ; as to putting,
judging purely by this day's play one would
call her a bad approach putter and a good holer-

out. At the 7th and 8th holes in the morning round she was terribly ill-advised to attempt the long carry over the cross bunker with her second shot, and in the afternoon round she made the very same fatal mistake at the 7th hole.

Taking the day's play as a whole, Mr. Hilton did not do himself quite justice. For 14 holes in the morning he played beautifully, hitting the ball crisply and firmly, never trying for great length, but playing the holes steadily and well in the proper number. He then made a slip or two; but his score of 78, with a fair breeze blowing and tees very far back, was a good one. In the afternoon he played thoroughly bad golf for the first 9 holes, his long game being very erratic and his putting weak. He came back in far better style, but he was not really himself at all in the second round.

The Second Day's Play.

If the first day's play was interesting the second was intensely exciting. It would hardly be too much to say that when there were only 15 holes left to play not one single one of the spectators thought that Miss Leitch had the faintest chance of avoiding defeat and yet she won by 2 up and 1 to play. A more dramatic golf match never was played.

Mr. Hilton stood 5 up with 15 to play; he was at the very top of his game, playing in an infinitely more convincing manner than he did at Walton Heath; it was a cold, windy day, making golf exceedingly difficult, and Miss Leitch had so far been putting very far from well. Taking all these circumstances into consideration, nobody dreamed that Mr. Hilton could lose. He began his own undoing by giving his opponent one or two chances, and she promptly took them and reduced his lead to 3. Then Mr. Hilton's golf became distinctly ragged, and he began to be short with his puts, which is always a disquieting symptom. Miss Leitch, meanwhile, had got thoroughly into her stride. Her wooden club play was really magnificent; for that matter it had been up to a very high level all through the match, but now she began for the first time to back it up with good putting. Mr. Hilton's lead melted away with that astonishing and paralysing rapidity which is known to every one who has ever lost a match that he ought to have won. Miss Leitch was only 1 down at the turn; then she was "all square" with eight to go; then 2 up with 6 to go. All this while one felt instinctively that Mr. Hilton wanted one turn of luck in order to "stop the rot" (cricket phraseology is often very expressive), and that if he could get it he might still win. Miss Leitch did not give him an opening, but he made one for himself by holing a long put for a 2 at the 13th. Now was the critical time, but Miss Leitch never wavered; she had victory in her grasp, and she did not relax her hold. Mr. Hilton had one or two very difficult chances, but he could not quite take them; his spurt died away again, and the match ended at the 17th hole.

If the Miss Leitch that the spectators saw in the afternoon was the real Miss Leitch, then no one in the world can give her a half. Probably she was playing just a little bit better than her normal game, just as in the three preceding rounds she had most certainly played below her form. She did 17 holes in 77 shots, on a long course, on a cold, wet day, with a strong wind blowing, and that is really good golf, no matter who plays it. The outstanding feature of Miss Leitch's game was her wooden club play. The tee shots were excellent, but the brassey shots were better. Time after time she hit the ball right home on to the green with a full shot; she never seemed to make any particular allowance for the cross-wind, but hit the ball right through the wind as Taylor does. Beyond all question her chief strength lies in these really wonderful shots. As regards iron shots, she is good whenever she can take something like a full swing of the club, and she can also play a low running shot effectively enough, but at present she seems to have little mastery over a pitching shot with the mashie. She putted really well in the last round, but she seemed to do so rather by virtue of courage and determination than of any great skill. About her pluck and match-playing qualities there could be no two opinions; she was really splendid. Not only did she fight hard when she was apparently sure to be beaten, but she never let herself be dazzled or upset by the sudden and surprising prospect of victory.

It would be very easy not to do Mr. Hilton justice. In the morning he played really beautiful golf, and it was a joy to watch his shots. In the afternoon he did, it must be confessed, partially break down, almost entirely upon the putting greens, but he had a very, very hard match to play. Nobody would have liked to have been in his shoes, and perhaps uncommonly few would have acquitted themselves much better if they had been.

THE TIMES BOOK OF GOLF.

THE MORNING ROUND.

The events of the morning round were so entirely dwarfed by the thrilling fluctuations of the second that they may be narrated very briefly. Mr. Hilton played almost perfectly going out, save for an iron shot pushed far out to the right at the 1st hole. He was out roughly speaking in 36 and yet Miss Leitch, who received her strokes at the even holes, stuck to him so well that at the turn he had only added 1 hole to the one that he took away with him from Walton Heath. The home-coming nine holes were very trying for Miss Leitch, who had to face not only a very strong wind, but a violent squall of rain that came on just as the players reached the 11th green. Mr. Hilton had two bad holes, the 12th, when he missed his drive, and the 16th, when he was trapped with a good second shot; otherwise he continued to play fine golf, and Miss Leitch did by no means badly only to drop two more holes. She would not have done that if she could have putted at all well, but time after time she overran the hole with her approach put. She erred on the right side in being bold, but she did err sadly.

THE AFTERNOON ROUND.

At the 1st hole after lunch Miss Leitch reduced her opponent's lead from 4 to 3. The hole is the best part of 500 yards long, and a cross-bunker guards the green. With the wind blowing strongly behind her she took the brave course of trying to jump the bunker with her second; achieved the " fluke " for which she played, and putting beautifully won in 4 against 5. She had a stroke at the 2nd, but here Mr. Hilton after a grand brassey shot holed a chip from off the edge of the green and thus won the hole in a 3. He also won the 3rd, when Miss Leitch missed her approach shot altogether, and thus was 5 up.

Now came the turn of the tide, Mr. Hilton taking three puts on the 4th green and Miss Leitch winning the hole with her stroke. At the 5th Mr. Hilton drove an enormously long ball and nearly reached the green, while Miss Leitch was lucky to avoid the heather. She played a lovely brassey shot, however, and halved the hole in 4. Both were in trouble with pulled tee shots at the 6th, but Miss Leitch's stroke gave her another win. At the 7th both were on the green in 2, but the putting was not good, Mr. Hilton being twice short in succession. The hole was halved in 5, and Mr. Hilton was thus still 3 up, but his putting rather shook the confidence of his supporters, and he did not in fact play well from this point to the end. Miss Leitch played the 8th beautifully, and won it without the aid of her stroke ; she also won the 9th by better putting, and stood 1 down at the turn.

The 10th was a most difficult hole in the teeth of the gale, but Miss Leitch hit three perfect wooden club shots, one after another, got her five, and won the hole with a stroke and the match was " all square." The 11th was likewise a difficult hole and Miss Leitch had no stroke, but she played it much the better of the two and won in 4 to 5. At the 12th there were played two glorious shots up to the green, Mr. Hilton's with an iron, Miss Leitch's with a brassey ; the stroke came in again and Miss Leitch now led by 2. The 13th was splendidly played by both, and Mr. Hilton, holing a long put for 2, won it and stood 1 down. The next two were halved by moderate but not brilliant play. Mr. Hilton had a put to win the 15th but did not hit his put quite firmly enough. The 16th is always a difficult four and Mr. Hilton's approach shot was not quite good enough; Miss Leitch with a grand brassey shot and a lucky approach—she came very near to topping it—had the hole in 5, won it with a stroke, and stood dormy 2. The way in which she played the 17th made a fitting ending to her fine round. She did not hit her second perfectly —it was a desperately difficult stroke—and her ball lay in the clump of fir trees to the left. She played it out beautifully, but was still a little short of the green, and then she laid the ball stone dead with as good a little pitch-and-run shot as the heart of man could desire. Mr. Hilton, who had pushed his second wide to the right, was left with a put of four or five yards to save the match. He struck the ball well and boldly; it hit the tin, but not quite the back of the tin, and jumped out again, Miss Leitch thus winning by 2 up and 1 to play. Her score for 17 holes was approximately as follows :—

Out—4, 6, 5, 4, 4, 5, 5, 3, 4=40 }
Home—5, 4, 5, 3, 6, 4, 5, 5 =37 } 77 for 17 holes.

THE OPEN CHAMPIONSHIP AT SANDWICH,
JUNE 29, 1911.

After a day of excitements quite unparalleled in the history of the Open Championship, Massy tied with Harry Vardon for the first place with a total of 303 strokes for four rounds.

It is almost impossible to convey the agonized state of mind of the spectators, who were kept running from one hole to another to see various players, who all at one time or another appeared likely to win. As a rule, after three rounds the Championship resolves itself into a duel, or at most a three-cornered fight, but here were six to eight men to any one of whom one little piece of good or bad luck might mean the winning or losing of the Championship. First of all, Duncan had the opportunity of a lifetime and flung it away by a too obvious inability to stand the strain. Then Vardon, with three strokes in hand, was favourite; he tried hard to throw his chance away and nearly succeeded. Next, Mr. Hilton came within an ace of winning the greatest victory of his great career, and, finally, Massy, by dint of a fine resolute finish, did succeed in catching Vardon; indeed, his last put but one trembled on the lip of the hole and he all but won outright. It really was a day's golf to shatter the nerves of players and spectators alike.

The Third Round.

After two rounds the number of players who had any appreciable chance of winning had apparently been whittled down to some half-dozen. Most of these were drawn to start comparatively late, but Harry Vardon began his round just before half-past 9. His score for the first two rounds was 148, four strokes behind the leader George Duncan. Once again he played thoroughly sound golf, dropping, as seems inevitable, one or two strokes upon the greens, but otherwise making very few mistakes. His one really bad hole on the way out was the 5th, where he took 6, to be accounted for by a pulled second shot, followed by some terribly weak putting. Otherwise he played very well indeed, and reached the turn in 36. Coming home he had another 6 at the 13th, where he played short of the bunker in 2, and took three puts. He holed a nice put for 3 at the 12th, however, and another for 4 at the 17th. At the last hole he sliced his second into a hayfield to the right and took some time to find his ball. He found it at last, however, and a good niblick shot and two puts gave him a 5 and a total of 75, which kept him well in the running.

Some way behind Vardon came three players in succession who were high up on the list— Mr. Hilton, Moran, and Ray, each with a score for the first two rounds of 150. Moran was rather unsteady, and did not do well; but Mr. Hilton played very fine golf indeed to the turn. He took 36 strokes for the first nine holes, and might have saved a stroke or two had he been bolder with his approach puts. He began badly on the way home by pushing his approach out, finding a bunker and taking 6 to the 10th. After this he played fairly good steady golf, and his round of 78 kept him well up among the leaders.

Ray might have had a fine outgoing score but for two dreadfully short puts missed on the 4th and 5th greens. The extreme shortness of the puts and Ray's very casual methods gave the impression that he hardly took trouble enough over them, but he is a deceptive player and probably tried hard enough in his own peculiar way. Up to the turn he did very well in spite of these lapses on the green, but coming home his golf was not at all good, and his score of 79 put him back four strokes behind Harry Vardon.

Meanwhile Massy and Braid, who with a score of 153 apiece for two rounds had a lot of leeway to make up, were both playing grand golf. Massy, who is inured to the gales of Biarritz, had been heard the night before to wish that the wind would blow hard enough to blow down every tree in Sandwich, and the wind that answered his prayers he certainly combated magnificently. There is no one quite so fascinating to watch driving in the teeth of a gale, no one who treats the wind with so splendid a measure of defiance. He finished in 74 and put himself perceptibly higher on the list. This score was equalled by Braid, but if he had been holing out well he might have done considerably better—might, indeed, have done almost incredibly well. It is true that he holed a long put for 2 at the "Maiden" and another for 2 at the 16th, but against these must be set some half-dozen missed puts that he might reasonably have been expected to hole. As to his play up to the green, it was magnificent— Braid at his very best, than which no higher praise is possible.

Taylor and Duncan with scores of 148 and 144 respectively started soon after 12 o'clock, being next to one another on the list. As for Duncan, it must be said that his out-going round was as painful a spectacle as is possible to conceive. To see a man palpably broken and hopeless is always unpleasant, and Duncan did break down most terribly. He took three puts on the green far more often than two, but this did not complete the tale of his misfortune, for he also played some very bad strokes through the green. He was very lucky to escape the bunker at the first hole, but did not profit by his good fortune and took 5. The second was played well enough, but a stroke went astray at each one of the next seven holes, mostly through weak play near the green. The climax came at the 9th, where he completely topped his tee shot, then proceeded to take a brassey out of a ludicrously impossible lie, and finally took seven to hole out, thus doing the first nine holes—byfar the easier nine—in 43 strokes. By this time the spectators of Duncan's disaster had mostly dropped away in despair, and perhaps this did Duncan good. At any rate he showed that although he has not by any means the ideal temperament for the game he has plenty of latent pluck, for he had the last nine holes in 40 strokes, a good score on such a windy day, and finished in 83, four strokes behind Vardon.

Duncan's total for three rounds was just beaten by Herd, who had throughout the Tournament been playing firm, confident golf. To a score of 150 he added a good round of 76, two strokes better than Taylor's 78, the two men thus making a tie for second place. Taylor played on the whole very sound golf; indeed, but for one serious misfortune, he should have been hard on Vardon's heels. He went out in 38 and came home admirably until he reached the 16th hole. Here he played a good tee shot, the ball being straight past the hole on high ground at the top of the green. His first put was far too hard; he failed to lay the next one dead, and holed out in 5, having taken four puts on this one fatal green.

THE FINAL ROUND.

Exciting as had been the play in the morning, it was positively dull compared with that of the afternoon. There were some eight men, any one of whom had a good chance of winning, and nearly every one of then at one time seemed likely to do so. Harry Vardon, with his lead of three strokes, was naturally a strong favourite, and he was the first to start. He reached the turn in 38, a fair but by no means reassuring score, and then he proceeded to hurl away his chances in the most lamentable manner. His score of 6, 5, 5 for the first three homeward holes was as bad as need be, but afterwards he steadied down and did well to have a total no higher than 80. His score for four rounds was therefore 303, and his competitors were thenceforward set a definite task.

The first real thrill of the afternoon—indeed, the most thrilling moment of the whole meeting —arrived when the rumour flew across the links that Mr. Hilton had reached the turn by magnificent golf in 33 strokes. Thus by the time the turn was reached he had wiped off his deficit of 5 strokes to Vardon. The glorious possibility of an amateur once again winning was enough to send the crowd scampering across the course in the wildest excitement. Two 4's was a fine beginning of the homeward half, but then came the first disaster—a 6 at the 12th hole. Here Mr. Hilton was very unlucky in being trapped off a fine tee shot. Even so he lay apparently stone dead in 4, but missed a very short put. The next two holes were grandly played in 4 and 5, and there was nothing to complain of in a 5 at the 15th, but the 16th provided the second and final disaster. He pulled his tee shot into a bunker, hit out rather too far, did not get his third dead, and took 5 to the hole. This was practically the end of him, for the last two holes are terribly difficult 4's against the wind. Mr. Hilton took two 5's, and so finished one stroke behind Vardon.

Next came Ray, who by the time the turn was reached appeared to have lost all hope. However, he started homeward so brilliantly with 3, 4, 3 that he had quite a good chance, His spurt died away, however, at those three punishing long holes, and he finished well up, but not quite well enough.

Even now there were no fewer than five possible winners left—Braid, Massy, Duncan, Taylor, and Herd, of whom the last named was the earliest starter. He went out in 36, but then came two fatal 5's, which ought to have been 4's, at the 11th and 12th. After those two holes all is hard fighting and chances of 4's are few. Still, Herd made a gallant struggle, and when he teed his ball for the last hole he needed a 4 to beat Vardon. He hooked his drive into the rough and was ultimately left with a put of some 9ft. to tie. He struck the ball perfectly and it went right into the hole, only to hop out again, and Vardon could for the moment breathe freely once more.

At this point, however, came reports of great play on the part of Massy, and the now exhausted spectators rushed out once more to find the Frenchman left with 12 strokes for the last three holes to tie with Vardon. He played the 16th perfectly, very nearly holing his put for 2, and then came the most crucial 17th—a very difficult hole against the wind. He hit a grand drive and then had to wait a long time before playing. His second shot when it came was neither good nor bad; he was some way short of the green in 2 and holed out in 5. Now he had to do the last hole in 4 in order to tie. A splendid tee shot left him with rather a nasty lie under the face of the hill. He took some lofted wooden club and hit a lovely shot straight on to the green about 12 yards short of the hole. The put was not a pleasant one, for the ball had to climb a hill, but he struck it perfectly, laid it stone dead, and holed out in 4 amid loud and well-deserved cheering.

Duncan, Taylor, and Ayton were still left, all three possessing a distinct chance. Duncan hurled it away by again playing very badly for the first nine holes. Taylor, who had no luck on the greens, went out in 37, but he started home with a 5, and a 6 at the 12th hole finally extinguished any real chance. Ayton's hope was at the best rather a forlorn one ; except for two bad holes he played good golf, but not quite good enough, and so Massy and Vardon were left at the head of the list.

The tie was played off on the following day, when Vardon played magnificent golf and won easily, Massy giving up the struggle at the 35th hole.

Braid v. Ray.

Final of *News of the World* Tournament at Walton Heath, October 5, 1911.

After a desperate struggle Braid beat Ray by 1 hole at Walton Heath and so won the *News of the World* Tournament for the fourth time.

It was a match of really extraordinary vicissitudes. The morning's play, although excellent and interesting, was comparatively uneventful, Braid being left with a lead of 1 hole. The first two holes in the afternoon were halved, and then came one of those crucial holes upon which the fate of a match so often turns. Ray, having apparently the best of the hole and with a simple pitch to play, topped his ball into a bunker and lost the hole. He was clearly upset by this mishap, and for the next six holes played very feebly. Braid, quick to take advantage, played magnificent golf, won hole after hole, and turned 6 up, a position apparently unassailable. Then the tide began to turn and Ray won two holes back out of the next four. Still he was 4 down with 5 to play, and no one dreamed that the match could go to the last hole. Braid, however, proceeded to take no fewer than four puts on the 14th green; he lost the hole and with it for once in a way something of his wonderful imperturbability. From that moment Ray the pursuer had Braid the fugitive on the run, and harried him most unmercifully, so that the partisans of Walton Heath heaved a very genuine sigh of relief when Braid holed his last put, 6in. long, and won by a single hole. Although he just failed to win Ray made the most gallant fight conceivable, and his play for the last nine holes was the more praiseworthy because for a few holes on the way out he had so palpably "cracked."

Some very fine driving was only to be expected between two such mighty hitters, and a good many people fancied that in the matter of length Ray would have something the best of it. They proved to be quite wrong, however, for alike in length and direction Braid was on the day beyond all doubt the finer hitter of the two. He was driving a grand low-flying ball with just a suspicion of hook which travelled splendidly through the wind. On the whole his putting was also better than that of Ray, for, although he made one or two grievous errors, he holed a number of exceedingly useful puts. Ray, on the other hand, never seemed at all comfortable on the greens, and rang the changes on his aluminium and iron putters with a frequency which neither bespoke nor inspired confidence.

If, then, Braid had the better both of the driving and putting it may be asked why he did not win more easily. The right answer probably is that when he did make a mistake it was of a more disastrous nature than those of his opponent. Two or three times he followed up one bad stroke by another still worse in a way not at all characteristic of him. He thus lost holes which he ought not only to have halved, but to have won outright, and one or two mistakes of this kind are apt to be terribly expensive.

The story of the whole match is one of mistakes and recoveries, and not of faultless play; but lest it may seem that too much stress is laid on the mistakes and too little on the many fine strokes, it should be said at once that when the wind and rain, the length of the course, and the strenuous character of the struggle are taken into consideration the golf was on the whole very fine indeed.

The First Round.

Ray took the lead at the first hole, where Braid hooked into a bunker from the tee; the second and third were halved, Ray making a magnificent pitch out of a rut at the third. At the fourth hole he laid a very long iron shot out of the rough stone dead and stood 2 up, only to lose his advantage at once through Braid playing the next two holes to perfection in 3 and 2 respectively. The 7th was halved, but at the 8th Ray made various mistakes and took 6 to Braid's 4. Braid was thus 1 up and had a grand chance of winning the 9th when Ray pulled his second into the rough to the left of the green. Braid, however, pulled his shot to almost exactly the same spot, and the hole was halved in a rather ignominious 6. At the 10th Ray played a perfect run up, got his 3, and squared the match, but then lost the next three holes in succession.

At about this point a violent downpour of bitterly cold rain came on, and Ray for a while seemed prejudicially affected by it, whereas Braid played the 11th, 12th, and 13th just as well as they could humanly be played. Braid was now 3 up with 5 to go on the morning's play, but just when he might have pressed home his attack and secured a big lead he gave a really astonishing display of bad putting, and lost the 14th hole, which Ray also had played quite poorly. At the 15th Braid holed a long curly downhill put for a 4, and halving the 16th stood 3 up with 2 to play. An almost unplayable lie in the heather, however, lost him the 17th, and Ray also won the 18th in a fine 3, thus finishing only 1 down.

The scores were approximately as follows, though it should be said that to give Braid a 6 at the 17th hole is somewhat generous, as he might very well have taken 7.

BRAID.

Out—5, 4, 4, 5, 3, 2, 4, 4, 6=37 } 75
Home—4, 4, 3, 3, 6, 4, 4, 6, 4=38 }

RAY.

Out—4, 4, 4, 3, 4, 3, 4, 6, 6=38 } 75
Home—3, 5, 4, 4, 5, 5, 4, 4, 3=37 }

THE SECOND ROUND.

The second round opened with two steady halves in 4 and 5. At the third Ray drove straight down the course, while Braid rather sliced his ball so that it lay awkwardly tucked up behind the bank of a bunker and unpleasantly close to the railings. Ray, however, topped his ball straight along the ground into the bunker, while Braid played a lovely shot out of his difficulties, winning the hole easily and standing 2 up again. Then began a time of sore tribulation for Ray. He was weak all the way to the 4th hole, took three puts, and lost it in 6 to 5. At the next two holes he was well on the green with his tee shots, but putted in a very half-hearted manner; he was wofully short with his approach puts, and made two very poor efforts at holing out. At the 7th he pulled himself together and got a fine 4, but Braid, with a terrific brassey shot, laid his ball five yards from the hole and holed his put for a 3, and thus became 6 up. Braid took three puts on the 8th green and Ray did exactly the same thing on the 9th, so that Braid's lead of 6 was still unimpaired at the turn.

Then began Ray's spurt, so well sustained, so brilliant, and so courageous as to challenge comparison with anything ever seen in a big match. He won the 10th in 3 to 4, halved the 11th, and won the short 12th in 3 to 4, Braid being bunkered from the tee. At the 13th Ray played a gorgeous approach shot and laid his ball as near dead as might be, but he never came within inches of holing his put, dragging the ball right across the hole. Thus Braid was still 4 up with 5 to play, and he had rather the better of the 14th hole, being on the green in 2 while Ray was over in the rough grass. Braid had putted badly at this same hole in the morning, but he putted a great deal worse in the afternoon; four puts did he take, and Ray won the hole with a very mediocre 5.

Worse, if possible, was to come at the 15th hole. Both were some little distance short in 2, and Ray had to play the odd. He played rather a feeble run up, and his ball lay some 15 yards short of the hole, and that on a treacherous sloping green; indeed, he seemed by no means

certain of getting a 5. Braid had an easy enough
pitch to play over a bunker, but he pitched the
ball far too short, right into the middle of the
bunker. He got out very well, but Ray, not
to be denied, ran down his long and curly put
for 4, and was now only 2 down with 3 to play.

Braid's position was not by any means so
pleasant as it had been a few holes before, but
his troubles seemed at an end when Ray sliced
into a bunker, while he himself hit a grand shot
right down the course. Ray's ball lay quite
close to the face, but with a truly heroic effort
he nearly reached the green, played a good run
up, and holing out firmly and well, got a hard
half in 4—Braid dormy 2. Both made splendid
seconds to the 17th hole, more especially Braid,
who had to play out of heather. Neither of
them was on the green, but Braid was a good deal
the nearer of the two. Ray ran his ball up to
within some 7ft. or 8ft. ; Braid, electing to play
with his aluminium putter, a club which he had
not touched throughout the Tournament, was
very short indeed. He just failed to get his 4 :
Ray ran down his put, by no means an easy one
under any circumstances, and won the hole—
Braid dormy 1.

Both had fine drives to the last hole, and Ray,
playing the odd, was within 10 or 12 yards of
the hole. Braid played another grand shot,
and was some 4 yards nearer. Ray's one hope
clearly lay in holing his long put, for the green
is a flat and easy one, and Braid could hardly by
any stretch of imagination take more than two
puts. He took plenty of time, and hit the ball
beautifully clean, but it never looked like being
quite up from the moment it left the club, and
stopped 3 inches short. Braid made no mistake ;
laid his ball within 6 inches or so, and then, holing

out, won a match that will not easily be forgotten
by any one who saw it. The scores were :—

BRAID.

Out—4, 5, 4, 5, 3, 3, 3, 5, 4 = 36 }
Home—4, 4, 4, 4, 6, 6, 4, 5, 4 = 41 } 77

RAY.

Out—4, 5, 5, 6, 4, 4, 4, 4, 5 = 41 }
Home—3, 4, 3, 4, 5, 4, 4, 4, 4 = 35 } 76

MR. JOHN BALL v. MR. ABE MITCHELL.

Final of the Amateur Championship at Westward Ho! June 7, 1912.

Mr John Ball beat Mr. Abe Mitchell at the
38th hole in the final match of the Amateur
Championship at Westward Ho! and so became
Champion for the eighth time.

Mr. Ball won by playing for the most part
masterly golf, and, above all, by an exhibition
of dogged determination such as he has never
excelled. He may have played better golf in his
younger days, but more plucky golf never.
Nor was his opponent in the least behind him
in this respect. Mr. Mitchell, more especially
in the second round, showed that he possesses
fighting qualities of the very highest kind. He
stood 3 holes up at the end of the first round.
He lost all his lead in the first 5 holes in the
afternoon, and yet he never showed any signs
of "cracking." Indeed, so finely did he play
that, could he have holed a straightforward
put of between 4ft. and 5ft. on the last green,
he would have won the match. He missed that
put and finally threw away his chance by completely topping his drive to the second additional
hole; but nearly all his golf, played under
severest possible strain, was beyond praise.

135

THE TIMES BOOK OF GOLF.

The excitement was, of course, intense; indeed one of the few final ties which can be compared to this one was that between Mr. Ball and Mr. Tait at Prestwick in 1899, when Mr. Ball, after having been 3 down at the end of the first round, snatched just such another wonderful match out of the fire.

In one respect the excitement was unpleasantly great. A section of the local spectators, having conceived a violent liking for Mr. Mitchell, behaved very badly, and once or twice, to their eternal disgrace, applauded loudly when Mr. Ball missed a put. It is a long time since one can remember so venomous and unsportsmanlike a crowd at a golf match. It was the very last form of partisanship that Mr. Mitchell himself would approve, and it probably did him a very great deal more harm than good, while the effect on Mr. Ball (if anything can have any effect at all on those nerves of iron) would merely be to rouse him into trying harder than ever.

The First Round.

The 1st hole supplied a good illustration of the value of Mr. Mitchell's tremendous power. Mr. Ball hit two fine shots with a wooden club dead on the flag, and was a little short of the green; Mr. Mitchell only needed an iron club to get home in 2; as a matter of fact he did not hit his second quite perfectly, and the hole was halved in 5. At the 2nd Mr. Ball topped his brassey shot and Mr. Mitchell won in 4 to 5. He also won the 3rd, where Mr. Ball again topped his second, this time with a cleek, and was bunkered. At the 4th Mr. Mitchell, for once in a way, hit a poor tee shot, found his ball lying heavily, and lost the hole in 6 to 4. He won the 5th with a beautifully-played 2, but was again in trouble from the tee going to the 6th and lost *the hole. Mr. Ball was now 1 down, but his* **drive at the** 7th hole, although by no means a **bad one, was** not quite *long enough to carry* the bunker, and Mr. Mitchell won comfortably. The short 8th was ingloriously played by both parties. Mr. Mitchell hooked, and Mr. Ball sliced ; the latter elected to play his second over the bunker with his usual audacity and a straight-faced iron from a position where any other man in the world would have taken a niblick, a club that Mr. Ball does not trouble even to carry in his bag. For once he failed ; he " fluffed " the ball into the bunker, failed to get out with his next stroke, and lost the hole. He seemed likely to lose the 9th as well, where Mr. Mitchell made an enormous shot from the tee. Instead of playing safely to the right, however, Mr. Mitchell imprudently went straight for the green, was caught in a little pot bunker, putted indifferently, and lost the hole. Mr. Mitchell was thus 2 up at the turn, having gone out in the very moderate score of 42.

At the 10th Mr. Ball played a lovely second stroke to within seven feet of the pin. His put for a 3 went in and out of the hole, but he was laid practically a dead stymie. He got his next put down, but could not avoid knocking in Mr. Mitchell's ball as well, and the hole was halved. Two more good halves followed, and then to the 13th Mr. Ball played a peerless brassey shot, such as no one else can hit, straight as a line the whole way, laying the ball six yards from the hole. He won the hole in 4 to 5, and was again only 1 down.

Then came a very critical hole, the short 14th. Mr. Mitchell's ball was 15 yards from the hole after two strokes and he seemed likely to take 5 ; Mr. Ball with his tee shot lay in a bunker in front of the green. Once again he took the same straight-faced iron club, when anybody else would have used a niblick. Even with this unusual weapon he is usually one of the surest players out of sand, but this time he made a complete failure of the stroke, took 3 to get out, and gave up the hole. This was a terrible blow, and worse was to come, for Mr. Ball laid himself a dead stymie at the 15th, and was very short going to the 16th. He lost both holes and stood 4 down with 2 to play. Mr. Mitchell made his opponent a present of the 17th by surprisingly bad putting, but he managed to halve the 18th after having escaped the burn only by the skin of his teeth. He thus finished the first round 3 up. The scores, which can only be given very roughly, were as follows :—

MR. MITCHELL.

Out—5, 4, 5, 6, 2, 6, 4, 4, 6=42 } 80
Home—4, 4, 4, 5, 4, 4, 3, 6, 4=38 }

MR. BALL.

Out—5, 5, 6, 4, 3, 4, 5, 6, 5=43 } 83
Home—4, 4, 4, 4, 6, 5, 4, 5, 4=40 }

THE SECOND ROUND.

It was felt by every one that the first two holes of the second round were all-important to Mr. Ball. The holes are of just such a length as to give Mr. Mitchell a commanding advantage, and if he could win them he would have such a lead as to be practically sure of victory. He did not win either of them ; after the 1st had been halved in 5, Mr. Ball played a truly magnificent second shot to the 2nd hole and won it in 4 to 5. The 3rd was halved, but Mr. Ball, with a good put, lopped off another hole at the 4th. At the 5th the spectators, who were not very well managed, crowded far too close to the green. Mr. Ball played first; his ball bounded over the green, hit a spectator, and cannoned back clear of a bunker on to the green; Mr. Mitchell's ball, on the other hand, hit another spectator and fell into the bunker. It was exceedingly hard on Mr. Mitchell, who thus lost the last hole of his lead of three. However, he never showed any signs of faltering and played the next two holes perfectly in 4 each, halving one and winning the other. The 8th Mr. Ball won in a splendid 2, but he came completely to grief at the 9th, and Mr. Mitchell, who also played this hole very shakily, was 1 up at the turn.

The play now began to grow more and more thrilling at every hole. First, Mr. Mitchell drove into rushes at the 10th, played out, and snatched a wonderful half by means of a long put. Then Mr. Ball hooked into rushes at the 11th and seemed certain to lose the hole, but Mr. Mitchell took three puts from quite a short distance away—a mistake which, in looking back, one is disposed to think lost him the championship. The 12th was halved in 5, but at the 13th Mr. Ball, as in the morning, played a marvellous brassey shot straight home on to the green, and followed this up by running down a long put for 3. He won the short 14th in another 3, and for the first time in the day held a lead of one hole.

Now was the time for Mr. Mitchell to "crack," if he had any tendency to do so, but he rose to the occasion and squared the match with a beautiful little pitch at the 15th. Both were bunkered going to the 16th. Mr. Mitchell's ball hung on the lip of the hole in 3 ; **Mr. Ball** was at least 5ft. away, and he had only about a quarter of the hole to aim at. By some miracle he holed the put, and the match was still square. At the 17th he made what seemed likely to be a fatal mistake, for he put his second into the big cross-bunker, so that **Mr. Mitchell** won the hole and stood dormy 1. Fine drives and seconds left the two balls nearly equi-distant from the last hole, some 15 yards or so away. **Mr.** Mitchell played first, and his put was neither good nor bad, leaving the ball about 5ft. away ; **Mr. Ball** played a beauty, laying himself stone dead. **Mr.** Mitchell had been putting very finely, but at the supreme moment he pushed the ball out two or three inches off the line, and **Mr. Ball** saved himself once more.

To the 19th both had good drives. **Mr. Ball** played the odd, a fine shot, but slightly sliced, and the ball went into the bunker to the right of the green ; **Mr.** Mitchell hit a terrific shot, but hooked it a little, and down went the ball into the ditch to the left. **Mr. Ball** got well out on to the green. **Mr.** Mitchell found his ball half under water in a deep ditch with a stiff bank in front. He played a magnificent shot out— a shot only possible to a very strong man— and excellent putting by both men halved the hole.

The end came at the next hole, and rather a tragic end it was. **Mr. Ball's** drive went straight as an arrow down the course, but **Mr. Mitchell** hit his ball right on the top and into a wet ditch. He got it just out, played another shot into another ditch, and finally, in trying to get out, hit the ball on to himself. This last event could have had no effect on the result, because **Mr. Ball** had meanwhile played another perfectly straight shot and had a certain 5 and a very possible 4.

The approximate scores for the second round were as follows :—

MR. BALL.

Out—5, 4, 5, 4, 3, 4, 5, 2, 7＝39 ⎫
Home—4, 5, 5, 3, 3, 5, 4, 6, 4＝39 ⎭ 78

MR. MITCHELL.

Out—5, 5, 5, 5, 4, 4, 4, 3, 5＝40 ⎫
Home—4, 5, 5, 5, 4, 4, 4, 5, 5＝41 ⎭ 81